TESTIMONIALS

"With so much already written about personal development and how to start a new business, nothing makes me happier than discovering information that is truly fresh, insightful, and transformational. *Ten Successful Start-Ups* will make a difference in the lives of those of us who dare to dream and believe in the beauty of our dreams."
—*Fanel Alerte, M.D.*

"This book is ironically timely in the wake of persistently high failure rates among small business start-ups, despite the proliferation of small business assistance programs and literature. Through real-life stories of successful entrepreneurs he has worked with, Harry Wells presents a compelling lesson on how aspiring entrepreneurs can successfully transform their ideas into viable business ventures. What makes this book really great is the apparent lack of agenda on the author's part. Avoiding the usual business clichés, Harry provides an objective and realistic road map of how to successfully start and grow a business in the face of risk and limited resources."
—*Clinton Daley, Co-Founder and Managing Principal of BizJump Consulting, and former Director of the South Bronx Economic Development Corporation*

"If you want a book that will give you invaluable experience from the business-people that have gone out and made their own success, *Ten Successful Start-Ups* is it. Harry Wells is a close personal friend who I have worked with on many different ventures and this is by far his best effort. No price is too high for access to the experience that can't be taught in a classroom. And I speak from experience."
—*Jason Safford, CEO, Safflyn Corporation*

"I am in my fourth critical year as a start-up contractor and I survived the start-up phase with Harry Wells's assistance. He helped me get my first loan and certification as a minority vendor to governmental agencies. I wish I could have learned

from this book in the beginning. The Esley Porteous interview especially strikes a nerve for all contractors."
—*Darryl Stovall, President, D&S Electrical Corp*

"In my capacity as one of the nation's top lenders, I dealt with thousands of small businesses and I found this book very enlightening. It is a must-read for those starting a business, or for any small business owner looking for tips on achieving success."
—*Mervyn Shorr, Former Senior Bank Vice President and Former NYC SBA Deputy Director*

"I met Harry Wells over 15 years ago when he was an aspiring entrepreneur and I was in charge of a loan fund set up by Corporate America to assist ethnic minority-owned businesses across the country. We have become close friends over the years and share many common interests, in particular, a shared passion for helping small business owners realize their dreams. Harry's book, a series of interviews with successful entrepreneurs who share their insights into what it takes to be successful, is right on. I feel that it is a must-read for any aspiring entrepreneur."
—*C. John Tear, Senior Vice President/Director of Business Development, Community Capital Bank*

Ten Successful Start-Ups

Ten Successful Start-Ups

How Their Setbacks, Management Strategies, and Practical Lessons Can Help You Succeed in Business

Harry L. Wells

iUniverse, Inc.

New York Lincoln Shanghai

Ten Successful Start-Ups

How Their Setbacks, Management Strategies, and Practical Lessons Can Help You Succeed in Business

Copyright © 2007 by Harry L Wells

iUniverse books may be ordered through booksellers or by contacting:

iUniverse
2021 Pine Lake Road, Suite 100
Lincoln, NE 68512
www.iuniverse.com
1-800-Authors (1-800-288-4677)

ISBN-13: 978-0-595-41430-7 (pbk)
ISBN-13: 978-0-595-85781-4 (ebk)
ISBN-10: 0-595-41430-3 (pbk)
ISBN-10: 0-595-85781-7 (ebk)

Printed in the United States of America

To my Daughters and their late mother

Hodari, Liana, and Kasey

To Angel Brown (a great editor and kindred spirit)

For your professionalism, enthusiasm and encouragement

CONTENTS

▼

FOREWORD by TAYLOR HACKFORD

When Harry Wells asked me to write a foreword to his book on entrepreneurship I was a bit confused. Why would a feature filmmaker be qualified to discuss small business start-ups? Harry reminded me of the many stories I've regaled him with over the years about my struggle to get films financed in the very tough world of Hollywood. When I thought about it, I did see a correlation.

Many of my feature films have been self-generated (*Against All Odds, White Nights, La Bamba, Blood In Blood Out, Proof of Life, Ray*). Even my films that were initially developed at studios (*Idolmaker, An Officer and a Gentleman, Everybody's All American, Dolores Claiborne, Devil's Advocate*) required a major quotient of my selling skills to get them made. Filmmaking is an expensive enterprise—requiring tens of millions of dollars to make and market a feature film, and the possibility of producing a "hit" is remote. Therefore, financiers are always wary about investing in a director's vision. Luckily it's always those very unique visions that produce the biggest hits, so the money people must listen to your ideas. How well you deliver your "pitch" is usually the difference between a "no" and a "green light".

The development of a feature film can take years. In the case of my film, *Ray*, about the legendary Ray Charles, the process took 15 years from beginning to end. Certainly, that was an aberration, but most self-generated projects take a long time to reach fruition. A filmmaker must have tremendous stamina and passion for a project to run that marathon. I'm sure it's no different for a start-up business.

The personal stories of the entrepreneurs in Harry's book sound very familiar to me. No one is going to hand it to you. You have to do the work and prove that you have a vision that can be successful. No one knows this lesson better than Harry Wells. Over the 40-plus years that I've known him, I've watched Harry disprove the naysayers and prove that he's got the goods.

When we first met, we were both freshmen entering the University of Southern California (USC). He was one of 13 high school All-American football stars and I was attending on a full academic scholarship. Because he was expected to excel on the football field, Harry initially focused on his athletic career, but his grades were less than stellar and it bothered him. He wanted to excel on the academic playing field as well. I pointed out that this was actually a good thing—it meant he cared.

After sustaining an injury that put him on the sidelines during his starting year on the Varsity team, Harry plunged himself into his studies, focusing on serious courses such as political science, sociology, and economics. His devotion to learning impressed his professors enough that one of them took him on as a protégé.

Harry defied his early critics and graduated from USC. He then entered a Masters Program and eventually pursued his doctorate in Economics. He later joined the staff of New York Governor Mario Cuomo and developed Incentive Programs for Minority Businesses.

In the 1980s Harry ran a successful import/export business, and today he lives in Brooklyn with his two daughters where he advises start-up entrepreneurs. Like so many Americans, Harry Wells knows that you can't wait for the good life to be handed to you … you've got to earn it. And he has.

Taylor Hackford
Director/Producer

FOREWORD by EDWARD ROGOFF

Entrepreneurship, which is currently the most prevalent business activity in the United States, is the backbone of the American economy. It creates new jobs, makes new technologies commercially available, and builds the big businesses of the future.

Although some people question whether entrepreneurship can actually be taught, a large body of research—and my own experience as a businessman, professor of business, and author of two business textbooks (*Bankable Business Plans* and the *Entrepreneurial Conversation*)—demonstrate that while nothing guarantees a venture's success, formal education *combined* with the informal education gleaned from the shared experience of others often makes a significant contribution to an entrepreneur's success.

Harry Wells understands this phenomenon well. His book, *Ten Successful Start-Ups: How Their Setbacks, Management Strategies, and Practical Lessons Can Help You Succeed in Business*, provides compelling examples and business profiles that will save you time, effort, and money before you ever patent your invention, open your restaurant, or start your consulting practice. It clearly reveals what is involved in the entrepreneurial process and it will teach you, the reader, valuable lessons about how to build a successful business.

I have known Harry for many years. He acquired the knowledge he shares here from personal experience, by starting his own businesses and by assisting other entrepreneurs with their ventures in his position as their Business Advisor. As *Ten Successful Start-Ups* vividly illustrates, entrepreneurs are an incredibly diverse group of people with a broad spectrum of motivations and goals.

Some people become entrepreneurs because they have to, limited by either economic conditions or by discrimination, as might be the case with immigrants who were professionals in their own country but find themselves offered only entry-level positions upon their arrival in the U.S. Such was the case with Esley Porteous, the Jamaican plumber profiled in *Ten Successful Start-Ups*, who worked picking apples before being able to start his own sprinkler business in New York. Many immigrants follow this pattern of using their education and experience as tools to begin or purchase their own business.

One of the most attractive aspects of entrepreneurship is the ability to accomplish a desired political or social purpose. This seems to be especially true for members of minority groups who view entrepreneurship as reflecting positively on their ethnic group and creating employment and other economic benefits to their communities. Running a business with both an economic and social purpose, such as a school or healthcare business, or starting a nonprofit organization to provide social services to members of the entrepreneur's specific community can achieve this goal.

Sometimes a lack of personal resources such as education, money, credit, and business network may actually represent a starting point for many entrepreneurs. They begin generating income through service work like gardening, home cleaning, or dog walking, and when they are ready to expand the business, they obtain training through entrepreneurship centers on subjects such as marketing and regulatory issues, which are often key steps in the education that leads to their success.

Often, people engage in entrepreneurship because they want to pursue their dreams, be their own boss, or develop an invention that will change the way people live. They might want to spend more time with their families, or structure their ventures so they have limited roles in the business, casting themselves as dealmakers who recruit others to participate in their ventures with minimal personal risk and commitment.

Being an entrepreneur can enable you to accomplish your own personal and professional goals, and *Ten Successful Start-Ups: How Their Setbacks, Management Strategies, and Practical Lessons Can Help You Succeed in Business* will guide you to this remarkable and satisfying destination.

Edward G. Rogoff
Professor of Management
Academic Director, Lawrence N. Field Center for Entrepreneurship
Baruch College, New York City

INTRODUCTION

In 1986, I was working in the Executive Chamber of the Governor of New York. My friends and family were speculating that I might end up in the White House, but I had entrepreneurial blood boiling in my veins. I quit my job and opened an import/export company.

Throughout my world travels, I had many unique and interesting experiences importing diamonds, housewares, and fabrics. JCPenney and Fabric Centers of America were my biggest accounts. I also worked with U.S. companies to export their products to new markets. I participated in international trade shows and developed a clientele base particularly in South America. Because I had developed a good reputation, other U.S. companies utilized my skills and network to conduct feasibility and investment studies in emerging markets. Before the end of apartheid, I represented a mining company in Southern Africa. I also participated as a member of a high-level consultant team that produced a study for the World Bank to build market share for apparel manufacturers in developing countries.

My journey was mixed; I lost and eventually made money. Like other college graduates and professionals, I suffered from beginner's grandiosity and cockiness. Imagine attempting to compete in the highly monopolized diamond industry! After losing my start-up funds and savings, reality sat in. It is now my contention that entrepreneurs learn more from their mistakes than they do from a theory-based academic foundation only. In my roles as a workshop speaker and business counselor, it is still a challenge to get my more educated clients to start and narrow their initial pursuits into more realistic, focused projects.

During my efforts to grow and expand, my wife died from cancer and I became a single parent of young daughters. Unable to travel extensively and sufficiently concentrate on business, I sold my interest and became a Certified Business Advisor. In this capacity, I have counseled and worked with hundreds of entrepreneurs, the majority of whom have been working-class immigrants and minorities. In addition, I have assisted in raising millions of dollars for their start-up ventures. I have also conceived and implemented award-winning entrepreneurial training workshops. Along with reading entrepreneur literature, my views on entrepreneurship have been formed by both direct and indirect knowledge.

The concept of an entrepreneur has evolved over time. In past schools of thought, an entrepreneur was simply a person with managerial skills and business experience who started a new venture. For a variety of reasons, they made the decision to take the plunge to become their own boss. Today's entrepreneurs are different.

While conducting workshops for the New York Department of Labor for downsized executives impacted directly by the World Trade Center disaster, I discovered that many of these well-qualified professionals were simply seeking economic life support. Thus many were not prepared for long-term entrepreneurship. In tracking their entrepreneurial progress over a three-year period, we found that their entrepreneurial zeal waned and the majority eventually returned to corporate America or to nonprofit sector positions.

In reviewing the literature, I found that present-day scholars focus more on innate entrepreneurial traits and states of mind. In McConnell's basic economic textbook, *An Introduction to Economics and the Economy*, "The entrepreneur is an innovator—the one who attempts to introduce on a commercial basis new products, new productive techniques, or even new forms of business organization" (see Recommended Readings). Thus the true trailblazer is a visionary, a risk taker who manages risks, strives for independence and personal achievement. For a serial entrepreneur, the journey is generally more satisfying than money, fame, or power.

The fact that successful entrepreneurs seize opportunities, mobilize essential resources, and build effective teams raises the question whether entrepreneurs are born or are the product of unique experiences and circumstances: Are the top-of-the-line business school graduates the next great generation of entrepreneurs?

In his dynamic book, *Copy This* (see Recommended Readings), Paul Orfalea, the dyslexic founder of Kinko's, puts forward an interesting argument to the contrary. He maintains that the 'A' business students eventually work for 'C' students. He attributes a great deal of his remarkable success to personality and character factors.

In my experiences as both an entrepreneur and small business advisor, it is evident that working-class and minority entrepreneurs travel a different path of development. According to Bygrave and D'Heill's book, *Portable MBA in Entrepreneurship Case Studies* (see Recommended Readings), the launching of successful ventures was conditioned by many common factors. The underlying thread, evidenced in their personal bios, was that the overwhelming majority of their study group was highly educated; most were raised in an entrepreneurial family environment and received start-up financial injections from relatives. They usually experienced the benefit of sustained training working in corporations and developed sophisticated professional business plans before starting their entity.

Among the hundreds of thousands of businesses that are started annually, there are many success stories of common, everyday people. Many faced steep learning curves and endured failure several times before getting to the Promised Land. They operated on shoestring finances and economic ruin lurked behind every corner. Most are first-generation entrepreneurs with little family support. In fact, they are burdened with the task of being a dominant breadwinner and socially stabilizing force. Many of their essential business skills are learned on the fly, frequently after near-fatal business experiences. The new-generation minority entrepreneur faces additional historical and political burdens because entrepreneurship is currently viewed as a means to collective economic advancement and empowerment.

The case studies that follow (which have been edited for clarity) are from numerous interviews I conducted with successful clients with whom I have had the privilege to work. Their businesses generate significant revenue and are experiencing growing pains. They constitute a gorgeous mosaic of women, minorities, immigrants, and white working class. Even though I was their business counselor, I often learned more from them than they from me. In most cases, our relationship has evolved into a long-term situation. I am on call for emergencies. We share ideas, books, and workshop presentations.

Prior to conducting the interviews, I developed an extensive questionnaire and then held lengthy conversations with each participant. Rather than compiling a boring regurgitation of common conclusions, however, I decided to concentrate on gathering unique valuable insights and lessons from each participant. For instance, my interview with an upcoming record producer resulted in what I hope is concrete direction and guidance for young people in the music field.

I improvised during the interviews and probed not only the participants' reactions as hard-core business owners, but also their personal fears and insecurities in the entrepreneurial process. The concluding section, Blueprint for Growth, synthesizes the mistakes, principles, and lessons learned into an action guide or road-map for today's—and tomorrow's—bootstrap entrepreneurs.

CASE STUDY 1: ROY SAWYER

INTRODUCTION

Roy Sawyer was born in Harlem, but has lived most of his adult life in Brooklyn, New York. Before his retirement, he was known as the richest African American in that borough. Roy started out by owning three taverns in Brooklyn and also managed five taverns in Manhattan. Later, he purchased several Laundromats, liquor stores, an office supply business, and a printing company. He also owned scores of houses, as well as a commercial strip.

Active both politically and in the community, Roy came out of retirement and presently serves as a Community Liaison officer for a local Congressman. In addition, he serves on various boards including the Greater New York YMCA and Boys and Girls Club of Eufaula, Alabama.

THE INTERVIEW

Background/History

Q: You told me just now that as a small boy growing up in Harlem you were very poor. How did you get interested in business?

A: Looking at other people, seeing how other people survived, how they grew up, how they were able to make it in this world, watching them discipline themselves, which is the most important thing—discipline. Saving. Not buying a new pair of sneakers. Not spending your whole pay, your total pay, putting money in the bank. As you say, looking for the future, not the present.

Q: Did your family influence you to go into business?

A: No. My mother was a housekeeper. She worked out in Brighton Beach as a domestic, making eight dollars a day. My father worked for the railroad. When they separated, I basically grew up with my mother. It was just the two of us. We lived in a room and we survived. But it was seeing how other people lived, my dream of becoming a person who would not have to worry about a dollar in the future, so that was my endeavor to move to the game, the situation where I would not have to worry about where my next dollar came from.

Q: Your family didn't assist you monetarily? They didn't give you any money to get started?

A: We didn't have any money. There was no money. Eight dollars a day, working two or three days a week as a domestic. Paying the rent, $16, $20 a week for the room that we lived in. There was no incentive. The incentive was my dream to get out of poverty and better myself. And as I said, I watched how other people lived, particularly white people because I was fortunate enough to work around white people. I went to school, I went to Stuyvesant High School, so I saw how other people lived. I worked while I was in school—in fact, I tried to work when I was eight years old. I worked in a candy story in which two people, Margie and Artie Shanaka took me under their wing because they didn't have any kids. They were the first people to take me to the dentist, and from there I did…you name it, I've worked it.

I have worked making Venetian blinds as a kid after school. I worked in a lady's glove concern during school. I worked from eight years old until the present. I think I was out of work maybe one month out of my whole life. And seeing how people—I worked for Carnegie Endowment For International Peace as a shipping clerk and I saw how people that didn't make much money, but they took vacations every year. They went to the Caribbean. They went to Europe. And I saw how they saved their money, how they lived, not frugally, but they lived where they were able to do things. And that was my discipline; that was my knowledge of watching them. And I figured if they could do it, so could I.

> *Cash is King.* Discipline yourself to save and you
> *will* accumulate wealth.

Q: So growing up in Harlem, which has always been a hotbed of different activities, different political movements, were you influenced at all by the teachings or legacy of Booker T. Washington, Daddy Grace, the Nation of Islam? Did anything like that influence you?

A: Well, I knew about Daddy Grace, I knew about Father Divine, being born in Harlem. Daddy Grace, I think, was on 125th Street and Eighth Avenue. I think Father Divine had a place on the block where I lived, on 128th Street. He had a place between Lenox and Fifth, so I knew about him. I wasn't influenced by them though.

My main thing was athletics, trying to get an education. I was very, by the grace of God, I was able to become an "A" student in all the schools I went to. I was prodded by a teacher, Mr. Markowitz, when I went to junior high school, to take the test for Stuyvesant, and I passed it. Got my knowledge in high school, and of course from high school I started going to college, but I couldn't finish, and I went to join the Police Department—I was 21 years old—and I was in plainclothes for three years. I was in the Police Department for eight years, and I was in plainclothes for three years and I was a detective for five years. I was never in uniform.

During that time, I saw how businesspeople were making money in Harlem and especially in the liquor business, in the bar business. I was befriended by one of the bar owners in Harlem and he taught me the business so I decided to leave the Police Department and go to start my own business in Brooklyn.

Q: So given your age, that would have been the heyday of the civil rights movement, when most people were concentrating on political action, voter registration, desegregation. You were not so much involved in that, but more involved in the economic aspect, getting your economic thing together. Maybe you could tell me about that.

A: I was involved in the economic part of life because of the fact of coming from a poor neighborhood, coming from a poor family. My main aim was to try to become economically independent and that drove me to getting started in business, leaving the Police Department and starting business because I saw how white people came to Harlem and they were able to become millionaires. And I said to myself, if they can become millionaires, so can I.

Q: So was the bar your first business venture?

A: Yes.

Q: And how did that come about? How did you get the money to become a bar owner?

A: Same way of saving. Being frugal, not spending money, saving money, and at that time, it wasn't, I'm talking back in the '60s, you didn't need much money to buy a bar. You needed four or five thousand dollars and I was able to save that money. In fact I bought my first house out in Hollis when I was 26 years old—a one-family house in Hollis. And as I said before, this discipline, saving, saving, saving, and not spending, which is the biggest part of people.

They say, when you talk about economics, they talk about how long money stays in the neighborhood. I remember reading an article where they said, in the Chinese community, money stays in the community six to eight months. In the Jewish community, it's almost the same. In the black community, money stays for like four to six hours. That's all the money stays, because most of the businesses that are owned in the black community are from outsiders. And when it gets dark and they close up, the money goes with them. So it was under that type of thing where I said, I know I could do it, and you have to believe in yourself. One of my mottos is, don't lie to yourself. Don't lie to yourself, and what are you bringing to the table. With those two things, anybody, not only me, but you, anybody else, can be successful.

Transitioning from Employee to Business Owner

Q: Tell us about the transition from being a policeman to being a business owner. How did you develop the skill? How did you actually learn to concretely run a business, i.e., a bar?

A: As I said, I was befriended by a bar owner in Harlem, and on my days off I used to go around with him to his bars. This was a family of Italian people that owned maybe 20, 30 bars in Harlem. The sons and sons-in-law, all of them owned bars, and as I said, I learned their technique of running an operation. It wasn't hard; it was just discipline. And believe it when I say to you: anyone, not only me with a little bit of knowledge, but anyone who has the willingness can operate a business, but they have to first get into it, study it, understand it, and then apply what they learned.

> *Find a mentor.* Learn from them to avoid making
> unnecessary mistakes.

Q: So how old were you when you started your first business?

A: With my first bar, I was 28 years old.

Q: You were 28 years old—a young man. How did you learn how to deal with your taxes, to follow your financial statements, to know how much money you were making? How did you actually learn to do those things? For so many businesspeople, that's rough for them.

A: You need an accountant. And you cannot put the money in your pocket. And you cannot spend. Discipline again. You've got to take a salary and you've got to stick to it. You can't—if you make a dollar, you cannot spend a dollar. If you make a dollar and your expenses are fifty cents, then that leaves you fifty cents. But you can't spend that fifty cents. The best thing to do is to take maybe five or ten cents out of it and live on that five or ten cents. That's the discipline. That's how you go into business. And a lot of people lose that because they take that money, they put it in their pocket, and money is a funny thing. It runs. It leaves your pocket; it leaves your hand in a hurry. You don't be extravagant. You don't buy the new car. You don't buy the new shoes. You don't buy all the jewelry. But you continue to live the small simple life, and you take that money and you multiply it, and you reinvest it. When I reinvested it, I bought a second bar. I bought a third bar. And I bought houses.

Managing the Business

Q: So it took you a couple of years to really say that you were on top and that you understood the whole bar business after coming from the police force.

A: No, because I learned it when I was in the Police Department—on my days off. I would work on my days off; I would go back up to Harlem and work with the bar owner that taught me the business and I would go around with him on those days. And I would watch him. I would watch how he operated and how he did his control, his inventory control, his monetary control, and it was just a matter that when I left, when I finally opened up my own bar, I used the same system that he used. As I said before, anybody can do it. It's not hard.

Q: Did you have anything like a formal business plan that was written down on paper? How did you do that?

A: No, it wasn't written on paper. Thanks to the academic education that I had in school and my stick-to-it-iveness, my no-nonsense way of living. It was these that I compiled into my way of operating. And it was just a matter of watching other people buy one business and then buy more and continue to buy every year, or every six months or seven months, take whatever net income you have and reinvest it. Turn it over. That's what my plan was.

Q: So you owned a bar how many years before you bought another business?

A: In three years I owned three bars.

Q: You owned three bars?

A: Yes. Right.

Q: What other businesses did you buy in your run? How many businesses did you participate in?

A: At one time altogether in the period between 1963 and 1972, maybe, I had owned three bars. I had managed five other bars in Harlem, all at the same time, so I had eight bars under my control at one time. I had, after the bar business, I owned a liquor store, I owned Laundromats, I owned real estate, houses here and in Brooklyn, about 20 houses. I owned a sporting goods store, which is John and Allen's Sporting Goods Store, office supply business down in the Brooklyn Navy Yard, which my wife operated, printing business, that's about it.

Q: One of the things I think a lot of businesses are facing, particularly with black businesses, is they need to grow. They're mom-and-pop companies but they need to grow. Tell me, concretely, how did you make the decision to go into a new business, a new endeavor? What caused you to say: "The time is right for me to expand. This is a good investment for me. This is the time for me to step on and do something else." How did you make those types of concrete decisions?

A: It was realizing that, if you're working in the community, there are certain businesses that have controlling interest in your community. At that time Laundromats were one of the controlling interests because a lot of people didn't have washing machines in their houses. So that was it. Or as far as sporting goods, sporting goods was a good business. The kids played basketball; people go fishing; people go hunting. It also included work clothes because people needed work clothes. Housing, of course, people always wanted and needed housing. So it was just what was needed in the community.

I stepped out of that role and went a little further when I start talking about office supplies. That's where I expanded out a little further because now I'm going into the outside world, not in the community world. So, the office supply business was open. My wife opened an office supplies store, which she ran out of the Brooklyn Navy Yard, and she was very successful. Also the printing business, of course, there's a lot of people need printing, invitations, political invitations, things like that, so that's when we expanded. That's when I left what you might call the "local" enterprises and went a little further out into the business world.

> Find an existing need in the marketplace and fill it.
> Customers will be waiting for *you*.

Q: These businesses—were they complete start-ups or did you buy other people's businesses?

A: Complete start-ups, from scratch.

Q: So when you started up something, what concrete steps did you use to build your business? I mean, there had to be some unifying formula that you used for all of them.

A: You know, when you say that, looking back, I really didn't have a unified business except my basis was I went someplace [and got experience]. I had a friend whose brother had an office supply business out in Long Island, so I went and worked for free. I went out there for a while and worked and learned the business before I came back and taught my wife the business, the office supply business. That's the way it is, you know. I did my, how would you say "your internship" the same way I learned the bar business. I interned at a friend's business, the same way with the office supplies, I interned there.

The sporting goods store was an ongoing venture. But again, it was in the same neighborhood that I had other businesses. It was a place where I owned a block of stores, I owned a liquor store in that area, so the sporting goods store was for sale and it was just another venture that I had within that little area where I didn't have to do too much traveling. I could go from one place to the other within 10–15 minutes—a half hour I was in each one of the stores.

Q: So you opened these new businesses, you had competitors, people always competing against you in one way or another. What kind of competitive advantage did you have over your competition? What made you more successful compared with somebody who might have stumbled along the way?

A: Well in the office supply business there was no competitor, no black competitor in the office supply business. It was different. We had other white businesses in the office supplies, but we had a niche that we went after: black businesses. Plus my wife was a woman minority business enterprise, so she was able to be certified, and since there were a lot of things starting at the time—a lot of our black CBOs were starting and struggling, so she was helping those.

Q: CBOs, community-based organizations?

A: Right. Community-based organizations. A lot of them didn't have funding, didn't have money for dealing with supplies and whatnot, so she was able to aid a lot of them, here in Brooklyn, to help them until they got funding. But again it's hit and miss. There's no great formula. You know, you're out there, you're building a business, you're doing networking. And word-of-mouth, that there's a black person that has an office supply business, you know, "I'll call them."

Then of course you get into the system of ordering, like everybody else, like Staples. Staples wasn't started when she started; they came in after she got into the business. But it's a business that you have to just stick to it and watch your "p's and q's" and follow the right formula. You know? That's all. It's just sticking to what you know best and learning how to operate that particular business.

Q: Well, each business has its own different dynamic: a Laundromat is different than a bar, is different than apartments. So each business is different. How did you learn the dynamics of each enterprise?

A: To a certain point, delegating authority. Take the Laundromats—I had four Laundromats at one time. So it didn't mean that I worked in the Laundromat but I had attendants in the Laundromat. My system was in the Laundromats, and I went to the Laundromats every other day to retrieve the revenue; each attendant had their bank, a money bank that they operated. So my job was strictly to retrieve the revenue, exchange their paper money for coin money which I did, and I had a service company that serviced machines, so that was basically it.

As far as the liquor stores, I had managers there who took care of the business and I was there in the morning and evening. It was a 7-day-a-week job. And from basically 5 o'clock in the morning till 12 o'clock at night. So it was long hours, but it was rewarding.

Q: Did you ever have any partners?

A: I had partners in the sporting goods store, yes. I had a partner there. Basically, that was the only partner I had.

Q: So you had all these different enterprises. Did you have a strong management corps or team that helped you run all this, or was it more diverse?

A: Diverse. Each one of the places was individually operated. I didn't have any assistant manager or someone who oversees. I oversaw everything. I was a one-man operation.

Q: And you did this for how many years?

A: I did it from 1963 when I left the Police Department to basically 1985 when I sold most of my stuff. Most of my businesses, and most of the houses.

Q: So that's like 20 years?

A: Twenty-two years!

Lessons Learned

Q: So in 22 years, what are some of the biggest mistakes you think you made or the lessons that you learned?

A: I think the only mistake I really made was not keeping some of the real estate that I had bought back in the '60s and '70s. I think that's…looking at it at this age, you know, the value of real estate now is up tremendously.

Q: Particularly in New York.

A:　Especially in New York. Especially in Brooklyn, here. I look around at the buildings I sold for $60,000 or $70,000 that are now worth $500,000 or $600,000—I look at that. But it's not a mistake because I made money. I bought buildings at $15,000, at $16,000, so when I sold it at $60,000, $70,000, and $100,000, I made a lot of money. But that's the only mistake. One location I think maybe I should have kept—the block I owned buildings on, Broadway between Stuyvesant and Myrtle—I should have kept those.

Q:　That's a hot area now.

A:　That was commercial. I should have kept that block. But what I did was, when I sold those buildings, I sold them to the storeowners. Because I said to them, "You have to be your own landowner. I'm selling the building and I want you to buy it, and I would work out any deal with you." And the deal that I worked out with them is I took back the mortgage and I told them they can pay me the rent, any kind of mortgage, any monthly payment that they felt comfortable with. And it didn't matter how long it was. So that's what they did. But that's the only thing.

Q:　Well, that was very noble of you. I've worked with a lot of different businesses and I don't know how a lot of these retail people survive because they're paying so much rent. One kid came to me and he wanted to open up a store on Jamaica Avenue, but the rent was 17 grand a month! At that rate, you're kind of working for the landlord, you know?

> Plan to purchase a facility for your operation. The Small Business Administration has programs (10% down payment, purchased building qualifies as collateral) for start-up entrepreneurs to purchase a commercial property that they primarily occupy (51%).

A:　Each one of the buildings, I sold. When I sold the liquor store, I sold the building also. There was another building I owned on Franklin and Lincoln, 6 families, 6 stores.

Q:　Franklin and Lincoln? In Crown Heights?

A:　Yeah. Well, I sold the building; I sold it to the person who bought the store. One I owned on Washington and Lincoln also. It was a Laundromat. I sold the person the Laundromat and the building. "Buy the building also, and I'll work out a deal with you." On Rockaway and Fulton. Another liquor store. I sold that guy the building, the liquor store *and* the building. Things like that, I don't know, because I believe that one of the criteria in buying a business is, you buy the building also. You're not at the mercy of the landlord.

Q: Right. That was much easier to do in your day.

A: So true. So true, because I was in an area where if you had a few dollars you could buy. Back in the '60s, early '70s, people didn't have $40,000, or $50,000, or $100,000. Even where I live now, my house, which is now worth about a million dollars, I bought for less than $100,000 back in the '70s.

Q: You'll sell it to me for $100,000?

A: No, no, I'll take the million!

Q: OK. So you are a community-based entrepreneur. Did you utilize a lot of government programs to enhance your business?

A: No, I did not. No.

Q: Were you very active in a lot of community organizations? And did that activism in so many different groups ever increase your bottom line?

A: No. Because at that point—I would say in the '80s—it was my time to give back to the community. The community has done a lot for me and as of now I still serve on the Board of the North Brooklyn YMCA; I've been on the Board now for over twenty years. And it's, although they say, 'Roy's Y,' which was right down there on Jamaica Avenue, I make sure that there is no child turned away, because when I was small I couldn't go to the Y in Harlem. I didn't have the money. So I went to the Boys and Girls Club. It didn't cost money.

Even now—I have a house down South and we started a Boys and Girls Club in that little town about four years ago which I go down every other month to attend the Board meetings to make sure that they stay on track. And I'm teaching them how to raise money, how to write for grants; to make sure it keeps going and isn't a failing situation down there. And so far in a little town of 13,000 we have about 180 kids who are enrolled in the Boys and Girls Club.

Leaving A Legacy

Q: You led right into my next question. While you were building your businesses, this empire, did you train your children to follow you? Did you build a legacy that your children now own their own business—are they entrepreneurs?

A: No, no. My kids, I have two kids, a boy and a girl. I should say a girl and a boy, because my daughter is the oldest, and my primary concern was to give them anything that I could possibly afford. And for them to go to college. They owed me an education. And that was the most important thing: that nothing stood in the way of their education. In other words, I didn't want them to work, I didn't want them to do anything; although my daughter, once in a while, used to come to one of the stores, but my primary concern was for them to get their education, to get their college education and thank God they have. My daughter is very successful as a teacher. She works out in Nassau County and I think she has two, at least two master's degrees. My son, he's a pharmacist, but he went back to NYU and got his master's degree and he's working as a pharmaceutical banker, so both are very well off financially.

Q: How have you built generational wealth?

A: They are heirs to my fortune; they have their own mutual funds and of course they are partly deeded on all my property that I still have. My grandkids have mutual funds that I started for them too. They're under eight years old right now and each of them has mutual funds, which, if we have enough growth—I have small cap funds, which have grown so far—by the time they get to be 20 years old, they will have over a million dollars each.

Q: I asked that question because a lot of entrepreneurs that I work with, particularly after they've been in business for a few years, want to start estate planning and planning for their retirement, so that's an important issue that comes up to people sometimes.

A: As I say, thank God that my kids are financially able to take care of their children. My wife and I…basically my wife is retired, I'm retired. I'm here, you know, on an annual part-time basis, working at this organization I'm working with now, not for the money but just to keep active.

Q: To keep the mind rolling.

A: Right. And it's my way of giving back to the community because I'm a Community Liaison, so I am involved with activities and problems of the community. If somebody has a problem with any of the agencies, I'm the one to deal with. I know a lot of the elected officials, and that's another thing. I mean, I'm very familiar with being part of the system before. And I'm happy. I'm happy doing what I'm doing.

I was on the phone with them just a few minutes ago, and when I finish with you I'll be talking to my Executive Director down in my town to see how they're doing because I'll be down there next week. I'll be down there to make sure that everything is rolling there. The kids, the kids. My thing now is children.

You know, we have a foundation for the children. I believe that you have to discipline, train the kids at an early age. I believe putting the best teachers in the early, pre-kindergarten to 3rd or 4th grade because once you've built that foundation, they have it. They will not lose it. My son says, "What you taught me in 21 years, I'm not going to lose it now." My kids don't smoke and they basically don't drink.

Q: You come from Harlem originally. Given all the regentrification there, if you were 21, 22, or 25 years old again, what would you try to do now from a business perspective? What do you see as an opportunity that would interest you?

A: That's a tough question. I probably would want to get involved more in the development, economic development. I think I would want to see more businesses owned and operated by the community. I would try to limit the outside influence.

Q: So you don't have any specific business that you would be interested in, that you would say, "Today I will go into real estate; I will start up a sporting goods store." I mean, what do you see are some concrete opportunities?

A: Taking control of mostly businesses, supermarkets. Taking control of the supermarkets. Taking control of the franchise businesses that have inundated our area. Things like that, you know. Keeping the money that flows out of the community within three or four hours right now—trying to keep that money in the community. Opening up, getting banks to come in. Getting credit unions. You know, starting credit unions, things like that. I'd like to see that we control our own area—see what kind of businesses that we can build, control, own, but ownership is the most important thing.

Q: We both live in Brooklyn. Brooklyn has the appearance of a new economic boom. How do you see black companies, minorities, being able to take advantage of the economic boom, not being left out, and being able to grow?

A: Being more vocal. Coming to the table. Putting what you have to offer on the table. I don't want to use the word 'demanding' but saying, "How can I share in the power? You're in my area; you have to let us share in what's going on."

Q: Right. I think that, when they talk about the impact of black businesses, too much is dealt with start-ups; you have to make your mistakes. But we also need to focus on people who have been in business for a few years, have a track record, and put our emphasis on taking them to the next level, from being a "mom-and-pop" to making some money. To grow from making 2 million dollars to 5 million. There's one gentleman I work with who is doing 3 million dollars here in construction, which is good. But if he was really organized and had a good administration he could do 10 million. Maybe we should be doing more to help the ones who are already out here grow, and then go back and deal with the start-ups.

A: You have to go to them and sit them down, and really understand for yourself: Is he willing to learn? Is he willing to take advice? A lot of these people don't want to take advice because they say, you know, it's hard for a person who basically has it made to take advice.

Q: That's a good point, a very good point.

A: That's what you have to do: sit down with them, put the plan on the table, and say, "This is what you can do within the next five years." That's what you have to do. It's strange that we have a lot of people who think they have it made. But as fast as you go up, you can come down. One bad decision can turn your world upside down. So you have to be disciplined in the way you do your business and make sure that you have your reserves in place—that you don't have to worry about the next dollar. That you can afford to invest this money over here. And make sure that it doesn't affect the money over here. You see? So, as you say, you're an advisor, this is the stuff you have to sit down with. But a lot of people are not going to show you their financials. That's another problem.

Q: I know. Most of the financials are in poor shape, and they can't give you an accurate reflection.

A: And they have to get some qualified accountants. Some CPA accountants who can sign their names as an auditor and not go back and say, "Well, you know I don't have the advanced degree, I don't have the CPA, I only have my BA." We have got to find them, develop that thing out—network with those people.

Overcoming Challenges

Q: So do you think black businesses still today are facing more difficult challenges than the average business?

A: Yes.

Q: What would those challenges be?

A: The challenge is getting the community to trust you. I remember a black grocery storeowner, people would walk by him and go into another grocery store saying that his price is too high. You've got to be competitive. You've got to have that trust from your community. Most other ethnic groups deal with their own ethnic group. You don't see a Chinese person in a black or Puerto Rican bodega. The person who owns any other business outside, you see them, but when they come into their business, they are carrying bags that they bought from their own community.

We have to learn to empower ourselves, keep our money in our community, buy from each other, buy from people who have interests in your community, not just a dollar. So many other ethnic groups have made millions, and in our community. I'll give you an illustration. I was talking to a former partner of mine, who happened to have been white, and his friend was telling him about why he is still in Bed-Sty. And I got a little frustrated with him and I told him, tell him this is where they started. The money they have, they made in Bed-Sty. The ring that their wife wears, the vacation they take, that money came from Bed-Sty. But at the same time, tell them that you have been here for 40 years in this community, and you are making money here. So don't knock someplace where you made your money. Tell them if it wasn't for Bed-Sty, they wouldn't be where they were. And that's the thing we have to do. We have to remember to take care of our own, because no other ethnic group is going to take care of us.

Q: What you said earlier was the money stays in the community for four hours? That's amazing.

A: All you have to do is look at the storeowner, where you are buying, where you are shopping, and find out where they live. They are not going to go to your store. First of all, they don't live here. They don't buy food here, and they don't eat here. So what is keeping them here? They are staying here because you are going into their store and spending your money. And when six o'clock comes or seven o'clock, they go and the money in their pocket goes with them.

Looking Toward The Future

Q: So what do you see are your future goals and challenges? What do you want to do with the rest of your life?

A: What I want to do for the rest of my life is just help our youth. That is the most important thing to me—my goal in life—to help the youth. If I can do that, I can see helping youth advance in education, staying out of trouble. That would be my greatest happiness is to make sure our kids do not get into the system. It's a shame that at this stage, people like you and me have to be the leaders of the community, because we have nobody in their 30s and 40s who don't basically have a criminal record. And that's a sad thing among us—that our youths have come into the system without really having a chance to do things to make themselves productive in our community.

Q: One of the young guys I interviewed does millions of dollars as an entrepreneur. So I think, if he could do it, many of these young people that you are talking about, they could do it too.

A: That's another one of my things. If I can do it, you can do it too. I have no greater skill than any other person out here. The only thing is, you've got to stick to it. You have to stick to your plan and don't let anybody deter you. The fact that you don't have a brand new suit, that's a material thing. But you've got money in the bank. You can go and call Delta Airline and say, "Give me a ticket."

I don't have to wait until I get a check or try to accumulate some, or borrow money. Do you understand what I'm trying to say? That's the difference between the guy who sticks to his plan and the guy who says, "I'll do it tomorrow."

Advice For New Entrepreneurs

Q: So what would you tell a young person, if a bunch of young people came to you today, what advice would you give a young start-up businessperson?

A: Don't think of today. Think of tomorrow. Plan for tomorrow. Plan for your future, because those days come very fast. You don't realize how fast they come. So don't put off to tomorrow what you can do today. Save that dollar today, save that dollar tomorrow, save that dollar every time you get a chance. And if you've got money in the pocket, put it to work, put it in the bank, put it somewhere. Don't spend it. Accumulate your wealth—everybody can accumulate wealth. It's the easiest thing in the world to do; you just have to make up your mind to do it.

Q: Well, I want to thank you for your interview. It's been very enlightening.

A: It's my pleasure.

SUMMARY

Roy Sawyer's successful journey as an entrepreneur, spanning more than three decades, provides many valuable insights about what it *really* takes to succeed in business. First and foremost is his philosophy about money: you can't spend every dollar you make. You need to save money by living simply, without extravagant luxuries, so you can accumulate wealth faster. Roy is also a staunch advocate for putting your savings to work—reinvesting your profits into further income-producing opportunities that will create a sustainable future for not only yourself but for your heirs as well. One way to do this is to buy the building(s) you operate from so you're not lining the landlord's pocket instead of your own.

In addition to investing his savings, Roy also invested himself, using his time and energy to acquire the necessary knowledge and business skills to run a particular type of company before actually starting his own. By wisely "interning" for others who were already running a similar business, Roy learned exactly what he needed to do to succeed also. In his words, no matter what type of business you're starting, you've got to "study it, understand it, then apply what you've learned." It might sound simply obvious, but it's often the obvious that's overlooked.

CASE STUDY 2: BART NACHIMOW

INTRODUCTION

Bart Nachimow grew up in the Brooklyn projects and was raised by a working-class Russian immigrant family. He graduated from the City University system and entered the information technology (IT) arena. After working for several firms, he started his own company with funds borrowed from family and friends.

Nearly sixteen years later, he is a survivor of the dot-com shakeout and the World Trade Center disaster. His company, MiBar.net, now offers computer systems and services to mid-size companies and employs approximately thirty IT professionals. Bart maintains that an in-depth grasp of his cost figures and manipulation of bottom line numbers were crucial to his success and survival.

THE INTERVIEW

Background/History

Q: Bart, tell me a little about yourself; give me some idea of your family background.

A: OK. I was born in 1954 to working-class parents. My father worked as a blue-collar laborer for the most part. My mom was a housewife. Never really worked. We grew up in the Glenwood Projects of Brooklyn—the East Flatbush Avenue area of Brooklyn, and we lived in subsidized housing. We were basically poor people. My father was able to get a loan from his uncle around 1965, '66, and with a VA loan was able to purchase a residence in Canarsie, so most of my life from 13 through 21 I grew up in a fully detached one-family house in Brooklyn.

Q: Are you the first in your family to go to college?

A: No, actually, my dad went to college; he graduated the University of North Carolina with a degree in economics, actually chemistry. He went to work with his dad on the sewing room floor and eventually became a foreman of the sewing room floor, but not much else. I was the second to go to college.

Q: What college did you go to and how did you become a 'techie'?

A: Well, I went to Brooklyn College, graduated in 1976. I became a techie basically through on-the-job training. I studied accounting—had a Bachelor of Science in economics. Then around 1980 or so I saw the movement from mainframe personal computers (PCs) to microprocessors and I had a feeling that technology would be affordable to small and mid-sized companies, so I thought that might be a place where I could earn more money than simply doing accounting work.

Q: So you worked for technology firms and then you started your own firm?

A: Correct. That's exactly right. I worked for a technology firm that was involved in hardware, a company called Computers Inventory Group, where we packaged large mainframe computers around tax shelter transactions. From there I went to a company called Automated Concepts that was involved in providing programming services to large Fortune-type companies. Basically my involvement there was as an accounting type, a financial person, but my intent all along was to use my financial background, my education, to leverage myself into a technology-oriented business. So it was a plan. I had a plan from early on.

Q: When did you start MiBar.net?

A: I started MiBar.net in 1991—July 1991—fifteen years ago.

Q: According to much of the literature I've read, a lot of technology people are very poor in business skills. How did you develop your business skills to become an effective CEO?

A: I think it was my background, the education I had. My roots are in economics, in accounting, so it was relatively simple for me to look at a balance sheet and/or understand cash flow. I think what made the business successful ultimately was my understanding of cash flow, my understanding of our cost structure and how to take that cost structure and to ensure that it synched up with our revenue streams.

Q: So why did you start MiBar.net?

A: Well, I had a vision—a vision that I could help middle-sized companies. I believed that there was a niche in the market that wasn't being filled, when middle-sized companies needed leading-edge technology. What I saw evolving in the networking arena with Novell and with Microsoft was the cost of technology plummeting, being available to small and medium-sized business. Technology that had only been available to large companies was now available to small and medium-sized companies, and I believed that trend would continue and that I could possibly hit a home run, take a company public. That really was the objective.

Financing the Start-Up

Q: How and where did you get the start-up funds?

A: Begged, borrowed, and stole, basically—well, I don't mean stole, of course! Family, friends, whatever money I had saved, my father, my mother-in-law, anybody that could really be around to give us the seed capital, I was on their doorstep, saying, "I've got an idea, I've got a vision. I think we can make this work."

Of course, I was a little naive in that I believed that customers would just come once we had the technology in place, but it was just a matter of going the old-fashioned route.

Q: How much money did it take you to start MiBar.net?

A: We started with about $150,000 in seed capital, which pretty much put us on the map. We opened an office, hired some staff, built, did a little bit of marketing, but basically it was just bootstraps. Just making sure that we understood that we had a limited amount of money and that we needed to make that money last.

Q: And did you get any bank financing in the initial stage?

A: Not at all. Banks wouldn't look at us. Being a service-based business, it was impossible for us to approach any banks.

Q: So you had $150,000, but how did you really start developing cash flow?

A: Well, the approach was pretty similar with our first clients, the same approach we had to raising money, which was, let's go to family and friends, let's see if there were any opportunities to consume our products and services in our most immediate circle, and there was some interest. We managed to bring in our first client, it was a good friend of the gentlemen I was working with at the time, and that was our very first client, so we started marketing from there and just building a client base. It was very tough in the early going, just ensuring that we kept an idea on our balances and lived as lean as we could.

Planning and Marketing the Business

Q: When you first started, did you develop an elaborate business plan?

A: I wouldn't say elaborate, but I had projections, solid projections. I had an idea of where the market was, but I did it off a plan. Most of it was conceived out of a need that I saw in the market for this type of technology and service in a particular segment of the market that was just being ignored. So I built some baseline projections, what I thought our revenues would be, what I believed our costs would be, and of course I was optimistic on the revenues, but not as optimistic on the expenses, unfortunately, so the plan didn't work. It didn't work out as I had anticipated, so basically we just had to hunker down. We had to hunker down and ensure that the money we had available would last us through our start-up phase.

Q: What is your market niche, and how did you decide on that particular niche?

A: We work primarily with small and medium-sized businesses, those that do between 10 and 200 million dollars in volume. And they are basically manufacturers, distributors, importers, retailers, pretty much anybody who is buying product or manufacturing product for subsequent sale to consumers, whether it's a business or a consumer end-user.

We focused on that niche basically because it was under serviced. There were tons of technology companies at the time focusing on the Fortune group where you can go in and make a living on an individual account. My sense was that strategy was dangerous because you can go into a GM or a MetLife at the time and make a career there but if you lose the one account, the business goes with it. So the sense was that we've had an opportunity to look at medium-sized businesses where we could not rely on a single revenue stream from a particular company, but try and diversify that revenue stream across many companies. That way, if any one account fell out and became disenchanted, or had financial difficulties, we would at least have a base of operations to continue from.

Core Services

Q: In reading your website, I was a little unclear. Do you train the technology people in these manufacturing companies?

A: We do a variety of things. Our practice is very broad in that we have three or four discrete components of our business. We do what's called platform work, or infrastructure work, where we go into a company and build out their entire IT infrastructure—servers, wide area networks, local PCs, printer configurations, that type of work. So we have an aspect of our practice that focuses on platform.

Then we have our most profitable aspect of business: delivering business management software to middle-market companies. Business management software is order processing, inventory control, and their accounting back-end. That's probably the most significant aspect of our business and it is the most profitable.

We also do custom programming for our clients, as well as custom Web development, so our practice is very broad.

Q: So in a sense, you train their technology people?

A: That's right. We become an outsource technology provider to many of our clients who can't afford the [in-house] expertise. Our staff is 25 people deep and they are all heavily trained, all Microsoft certified people, so we have taken the exams. For an individual business or a small company to go out and acquire all of the knowledge that we have in our organization would be impossible. So the concept was, let's be their outsourced IT department.

Q: So when they have any IT needs, they come to you.

A: That's the objective. As I mentioned, our practice is broad, so we can go into an individual account with any one of our four or five different products or services and they might only consume one of them. Our objective is to have them consume all of our products and services. So when we get into an account, whether it's on the business management side or on the infrastructure side, we'll always look at those additional opportunities, because the easiest sale is to an existing customer. It is far easier to sell something to someone who already trusts you and enjoys working with you than it is to establish a brand new relationship.

Q: What is your competition?

A: Well that's a great question. Our competition, probably on my block, in Manhattan, there are probably 10 guys who do exactly what I do, so it's a very, very intense business in that we compete with everyone from the large consulting companies, like Exentra, down to the individual guy that runs around with his cell phone trying to service every client. It's very broad, the competition. But I'm in an industry that is dominated by very small players. We are ranked in the top 50 in the nation for businesses that provide service to the small and medium-sized business community with middle-market accounting applications. So we are ranked in the top 50 and we're only 25 people. So a lot of small players, a lot of very small players.

Q: And what are the average revenues for these players, for companies that are similar to your competitors?

A: The range is very broad. I would say the average is probably a million. That would be considered a reasonably sized company, and of course there are the guys that are doing a billion. But the preponderance of the companies are a million and under. They are 'lifestyle businesses.' For the most part, what we find are competitors who are lifestyle businesses, where a couple of guys get together and they are looking to make a hundred, two hundred thousand dollars a year, and that's really enough for them.

Q: What is your annual revenue?

A: Our revenue this year will be in the five-million-dollar range.

Q: What is your competitive advantage against all these different players?

A: Well, we have a couple of different competitive advantages. Certainly, strength of reputation is a tremendous advantage. We have been doing this for 15 years. We've got a great roster of very satisfied clients. And essentially our focus is not on the technology; it's really on the relationship, to build a satisfied client. So we are very customer centric. What I find in most of my competitors is that they view their clients almost as a necessary evil, not as somebody who is to be revered. As we approach it, the client is the king. Our client is why we exist, so our focus is on client satisfaction. And beyond that, having done it as long as we have, and having a lot of people with financial backgrounds, not just an IT background, but financial backgrounds in the company, gives us the ability to take not just technology to a prospect or client, but to also take technology and business and the understanding of the processes that run that business. So we have a unique understanding of what they are actually living through.

Overcoming Obstacles

Q: So your company is 15 years old. In the initial phase, what were the major problems and difficulties you faced? I know money was one.

A: Well, obviously, the money was always the issue. There was never enough. And of course, building a deep enough prospect base. That's probably the second largest problem the company faced, in attempting to grow from a very, very small business into something more substantial as we are today was to develop an effective marketing program, to take whatever scarce resources we had and direct them toward client generation because ultimately it's about clients. We needed more clients. We needed prospects in our pipeline in order to develop a winning business strategy. So that was really one of the biggest obstacles we had: How do we develop sufficient prospects that would allow us to grow the business?

Q: But you, as a person, as an entrepreneur, struggling, what were the things that were really stressing you out? What were your major difficulties?

A: I tend to not stress out. Even initially, I tended to be very analytical in a problem. I have found that worrying was counterproductive, to get stressed over issues that were difficult, I always just looked for the solution and kept digging until the solution became apparent. And they weren't always apparent. I would do whatever I had to do, whatever it took. If I had to break open a piggy bank to make the next payroll, I was breaking open the piggy bank to make the next payroll. It didn't really make a difference. So stress wasn't something I tried to avoid. I understood the problems. I tried to put them into the right context.

Q: What were the problems in that particular phase?

A: Well, it was satisfying the clients, being able to deliver the projects that we won. And building a staff, because ultimately, it's about my people—building a winning team, getting my people to buy in to the philosophy, to the approach that we were bringing; ultimately to have that translate into solid client relationships.

Q: So as a more mature company, what are the major difficulties you are facing now?

A: Well, they don't really change. They just become larger in scope: How do we grow 20 percent this year, and how do we take the business to the next level? How do we attract and retain qualified people that can deliver the type of services that our clients demand? So the problems are the same, they are just on a different scale.

Money is less of a problem today. Since we run a successful business, we built up a reasonable cash reserve to allow us to not have to worry day to day about meeting the payroll, where's that next payroll going to be coming from, where's that next tax payment going to be coming from? So that problem has resolved itself. And it wasn't because we weren't worried about it or because we weren't focused on it. We focused on satisfying our clients, and we knew that if we understood our cost structure, and we satisfied enough clients, that the money would take care of itself, that the profitability would just show up in the bank balances, and it did.

Q: Two questions. Last time I was here, you had a crisis with a partner. What happened to your partner?

A: He's gone.

Q: How did you resolve that situation?

A: Just dogged determination.

Q: Because I know a lot of entrepreneurs, they start out with somebody and then they grow apart.

A: Yeah, he was around for 10 years and I knew it was a mistake from the second day we started together. Unfortunately I made a horrible decision that I had to live with for a long time. But it got down to the point where I knew what I was contributing; I knew what he was contributing. I knew I was contributing 90 cents on the dollar and only taking out 50 cents on the dollar and that just didn't work. So I made him an offer, a variety of offers, to try and get rid of him and unfortunately most of the deals weren't acceptable to him. Invariably it got to the point when I said, "Listen, I'm going to dissolve the business; I'm going to go to the courts and dissolve the business. I am going to ask for a judicial dissolution if you are not prepared to accept a reasonable buyout offer, and here's what I can come up with." It was the best deal I could offer.

Of course, I went to all the financing sources around, and most financing sources aren't interested in helping you buy out a partner. But I found a bank in Brooklyn, Community Capital Bank, a great guy, John Tear, who I was able to energize. Perhaps he was ready to be energized, I'm not sure, but he believed what I was telling him, believed in the vision I had set out for the company and he actually helped us get the financing in place in the form of an SBA loan for leverage, to get the partner out. So, he's been gone for five years.

We still pay a certain amount of notes, but by and large, we're clear of those. At one point we were spending over thirty thousand dollars a month paying debt service to this partner. We're down to about four thousand a month at this point, so for the most part, we're free and clear of that, and we just take capital and we're investing it back in the business in the form of our staff, in the form of our advertising program, marketing program. We're moving. We're moving to new quarters, new offices on Broadway. So we're just trying to take the capital that we're making and reinvesting it in the business. So he's gone. Thankfully, he's gone.

> *Give away money but not power.* Be very careful
> about bringing in a potential partner. It's better
> to pay someone for their service than to have
> their hand perpetually in your pocket.

Q: So what are the problems working with 25 to 30 employees?

A: Very difficult; very difficult. It's probably the most challenging, other than satisfying my 200 clients who are also very challenging. Everybody's different. Keeping them motivated and focused is probably the biggest challenge we have with our employees. It's tough. What we do is difficult. Our clients are very demanding and they tend to have a very high level of expectation from my people and the expectation—I have the same level of expectation—that they will deliver that level of quality to my client. So keeping them motivated, keeping them fired up. One of the things I tell my employees is that I want you to come to work every day fired up. I want you to love working here. I want you to feel like, when you get up in the morning, you don't say, "Ah shit, I'm going to work today." I want you to say, "Yeah, I'm going to work today because I'm going to make a difference. I'm going to make a difference to the company. I'm going to make a difference to the company's clients and to the company's client's employees." So I try to get them fired up so they see the bigger picture.

That's really the hardest thing—keeping them focused on the big picture and keeping them motivated to do their job. Of course, it's a small business. We can't compete with the large companies when it comes to consulting salaries. We do what we can but it's difficult. It's certainly a challenge. Recruiting the top people is very difficult.

Q: So do you have a lot of monetary incentives, retirement plans?

A: We do. We do have a great benefits plan in place for our employees. And that's really key. And also we create a great atmosphere for them. It's business casual. We do company events. We go to barbecues, baseball games as a company. We celebrate things. We make a big deal that this is a record year. It's a record year for profits and for revenues. We'll take everybody out for dinner and we try to just make it like a family so that everybody feels that they contribute. We have strategy meetings with different sections of the company, so everybody gets to feel that they're involved, also a good benefits program, competitive salaries and a sense of involvement. Their employment here matters.

Q: How did you survive the dot-com shakeout?

A: Well, it's interesting. We never really bought in. We never really bought in fully. What I saw as I was living through the dot-com bubble was that there was a lot of smoke and mirrors going on. There were a lot of transactions going down where the price tags were just unreasonably lowered or inflated. There was not much substance. My sense was that it was a house of cards. I saw it as the house of cards that it was, so we never really bought in. We tried to keep our business transactions rooted in sensibility.

That's not to say I didn't try to take advantage of that bubble. I tried to sell a piece of the company at that time and we were very close to getting a substantial cash infusion from a venture investor at that time, but then the bubble burst and all that money dried up, but our business wasn't really impacted dramatically other than the contraction in business transactions in general that went along with the recession that followed, but we didn't really buy in. So that's how we avoided the dot-com bubble.

Q: How did you survive 9-11?

A: That was a piece of work; let me tell you something. I had bought out my partner in March of 2001. I started making the payments to him on September 1, 2001, so the debt service kicks in and business dries up. So basically I went to my staff and said, "Staff, we have a problem, we have a serious problem. And what I need is for everybody to take a salary cut, immediately, that I can't tell you when I am going to be able to reinstate, because the economy is going to take a significant hit here," and they all bought in. None of them walked. And in some cases, it was 20 and 30 percent salary reductions. But we didn't lay anybody off. Our intention was to keep the team together, get rid of any excess staff that we had, which we didn't really have much of because it just wasn't a luxury that we could afford, but we just pared down.

We saw no new business activity for nine months after September 11. Not a single new client was added. And we were used to adding two or three a month. So basically we just got down to bare bones. We focused on our existing clients, servicing them like they have never been serviced before and our existing clients continued to spend. Our staff was willing to take the reductions, so we just got down to the base level spending that we needed, the minimum amount of money that we had to spend every month. There were no frills. People took the salary cuts. We cut back on benefits. We did what we needed to do to survive.

I looked for every dollar. I went to my 401K—I borrowed from my 401K, I took advances. I was going to make sure that we had the resources to get us through, to support the team, because of their willingness to get down. But ultimately it was our existing client base that enabled us to survive and my staff's willingness to take salary cuts.

> Take good care of your team and employees.
> They might just save your butt one day.

Q: When did it turn around and why did it turn around?

A: It took about nine months. I think the New York area was so traumatized, especially in small business. We represent a capital expenditure. Most of the projects that we get involved in are fifty, sixty, a hundred thousand dollars or more. So businesses just said, "Wait a minute, I just don't know what is going to happen here," so it took a full nine months for businesses to start regaining the confidence that we weren't going to be attacked again, at least not in a major way, that they could start to look forward.

The Federal Reserve did what they needed to—make money very cheap. The vendors that we worked with were offering zero percent financing on any technology projects that we were getting involved in. So I think it was a combination of the confidence of the consumer in the marketplace, the willingness of the banking system to kind of make money very cheap to stimulate business, and I think that's what did it. And of course my willingness to just continue pouring money into the business. I took no money out of the company for those nine months. Nothing. I lived off whatever savings I had. As I said, 401K, loans, credit cards, whatever I had to do. It didn't make a difference. It was a very difficult time. It was the only time I was really afraid as a business owner, because I thought the cliff was very steep and of course having just purchased the interest of my partner with a personal guarantee, it was a very scary time.

Q: Psychological trauma, or anything like that?

A: Well, I can tell you it made me humbler, certainly. I don't think I will ever forget that experience. I realize what my people did to help save the business. It wasn't *their* business. It was *my* business. But they were willing to take deep salary reductions, deep benefits cuts in order to help the business survive. I will never forget that. I will never forget the people; I'll never forget their actions, and I'll never forget the sense of hopelessness. Very scary, very scary.

Q: I remember, which I never understood, you applied for the SBA disaster loan. And I thought you deserved it more than anybody else. Why did they turn you down?

A: I don't know. Me either. I just kept fighting. It was just another obstacle that was put up, and I was determined to fight through it. It was just determination. It was a no-fear approach. I wasn't afraid, other than for going out of business for a period of time. But I wasn't afraid. I just knew that, whatever challenge was going to be put up, I would figure out a way to get through it.

Business Strengths

Q: So would you agree with me that one of the contributing factors to your success is your understanding of the numbers and the financing?

A: It's the only thing that made us survive. Technology is great, but if you fall in love with the technology, you can easily go out of business. What got the business to achieve a level of success was my understanding of our cost structure. If you don't understand it, if you don't have a comfort level with the details— that's not to say you always have to be immersed in the details but you have to understand the details—so that once you have that understanding you can then build a model to generate revenue that will support that cost structure. If the cost structure gets out of line, you know, no business is an island.

We charge by the hour. For the most part, we're a consulting business. Our rates had to be competitive. They had to be competitive, so without understanding the cost structure and the nature of what our rates had to be, I had to ensure that we were in balance. That was really the difference: understanding the way to match costs and revenues. The most fundamental lesson you learn in accounting is matching cost and revenues. You know, your revenues have to match your costs because if you are spending more than you are taking in, it's not going to last very long.

Q: So you are basically saying that unless you get a handle on the cost structure and how the numbers work, then it is going to be difficult for a business to grow and be successful.

A: There's no question about it. You can rely on advisors and you can rely on other people, but they are not around all the time and making moment-to-moment, day-to-day decisions. You've got to have that understanding. You've got to have that level of comfort. You've got to be able to look at a financial statement or a statement of cash flow and understand, because that's your business. It's a living, breathing—I don't want to call it a being—but it's a living, breathing thing. It has a life of its own. It's got energy from cash flow in and it's got expenses, and it's got to ensure that those are all in balance. They've got to be in synch. And you've got to understand it. Because if you don't, you can't make it. You can't make it, no matter how great your technology is. You can have the best technology company in the world. You can have the greatest technological solution. But if you don't understand that you've got to satisfy your clients, watch your cost structure and ensure that everything stays in synch with regard to inflows and outflows, what do you do? You just keep borrowing. You just keep going out and trying to raise money to manage your lack of business expertise. You can't. At some point that money is going to dry up. You've got to have a solid profit model. You've got to be able to sustain the business on its own. You know, banks are great. They can help you weather the bad times, but you've got to understand: the business has to be fundamentally sound, and if you can't understand that, if you can't grasp the fact that if the business isn't fundamentally sound, it doesn't matter how good the technology is, because if you don't have customers, you're going to be out of business.

> Control the numbers; don't let them
> control you. Learn to read, *and*
> *understand*, financial statements.

Q: One of my clients that I'm dealing with, her accountant just up and quit on her. He quit on her when the Internal Revenue Service was pressing her and threatening penalties. And what I was trying to tell her is that all these people who say, "Oh, I have a great accountant," need to understand that you can't just have an accountant; you have to know what the accountant is doing. You may not know all the manipulation and all that, but you have to know the basics.

A: The accountant should be there in small business to help you with tax advice. He can't help you run the business. He can give you guidance and input, but they are accountants. They are not businesspeople. They understand the rules and regulations for preparing financial statements and tax returns. So a good accountant is great and they might be a good sounding board but they are not going to help you set the business policy. They're not going to help you contain your cost structure. They may tell you that you're spending too much money but they are not going to tell you why or where or how to correct the problem. They can show you a statement that says, OK, you are losing money. That doesn't make them a good accountant, to show you that you're losing money. The entrepreneur has to understand: You can rely on outside people for advice, input, but ultimately it's your responsibility to understand how to make the business successful.

Lessons Learned

Q: So MiBar.net was your first business. After 15 years, what would you say are your major lessons or the major mistakes that you would sum up at this particular point?

A: Well, the major mistake initially was just being too optimistic about how quickly I could get the business up and running. And my sense that this was a no-brainer; can't miss. 'I'm hard working. I'm smart; I'm willing to do whatever necessary.' That wasn't enough. I have to tell you, that was the major lesson: You've got to go in with your eyes completely open. You can have a lot of confidence and believe in yourself, but you've got to be completely open to the prospect that you could fail. I never thought that I could fail. And failure was a real possibility at several points in the company's existence. Not that I ever wanted to internalize that but it was true. I was just overly optimistic in getting started. I really needed to start with a solid look at what the prospects are for the business to get it running, what do you really need.

Another lesson of course is the time away from my family. This took an enormous amount of energy and effort, so my kids are grown now. I basically was a weekend dad for the most part. I got in at seven in the morning. I went home at nine at night. So I lost a lot of time with my kids and now they're 21 and 27, and don't get me wrong, we have a great relationship, but those years, they're gone. You don't get those back. Those are the two lessons of life, which is to be realistic when you get involved. Know that it is going to be a lot of hard work, that there is the prospect of not making it. Frankly, more businesses don't make it than do. And it's really largely up to you. And there's really nothing you can't do if you want to, if you are prepared to do what's necessary, then you can get it done, but you just have to be realistic.

Q: Would you say maybe your greatest mistake was the partnership?

A: Oh, that was definitely a great mistake. And picking the wrong partner. Thank you for pointing that out. Yeah, of course. My background was business and finance. I wasn't a salesman. I knew that I had to have a sales-type person involved and this guy had a great story. He was very engaging. Of course, once you scratched a little bit, you realized there wasn't much underneath that. It was a mistake, a major mistake.

That's not to say partners are mistakes. But you have to make sure you know your partner so before you get involved, make sure the lines of responsibility are clear, and to the extent that you can avoid it, 50-50 is an impossible scenario. It could never be 50-50 because that's a guaranteed deadlock. Invariably, partners—whether they are best of friends or cousins or relatives in some fashion—are going to disagree. So you've got to have a working structure with a partner if you are going to have one. And there are definite benefits of having a partner. You get to go on vacation in a more relaxed way from time to time. Not that you get to go on vacation too much in the early days.

Q: So what's the second biggest mistake?

A: I think the second mistake—that's a great question—I think the second biggest mistake was early on in the business's development, I tended to delegate more than I should have, so I kind of took my eye off some of the details early on. Not the first year, but maybe years three and four, as we started to gain a little bit of traction, as the staff started to grow a little bit, I was starting to delegate, kind of removing myself from some of the details. It wasn't until I got back into those details that the business really started to grow and become successful. So I wasn't satisfied with struggling along.

My partner at the time was satisfied with the lifestyle business. I wasn't satisfied with the lifestyle business. I wanted to build this into a 50- or 100-million-dollar business. My objective was to take the company public or sell it to somebody for 100 million dollars at one point. That's where we started. That was the dream: sell the business. I see it happening all around me. We work in middle-market companies, so a lot of clients are entrepreneurs themselves. Many of them are in their parents' businesses. Many of them are entrepreneurs that started up. Sold for 10 million. Sold for 20 million. That's the goal. That's the goal.

Looking Toward The Future

Q: So your goal is to go from 5 million dollars in annual revenue to 20 million, 30 million. What concrete steps do you think you need to take to grow your business through the next phase?

A: Well absolutely we have a growth plan in place. Right now the target is to grow 20 percent a year, which we believe we can do and do reasonably, in a reasonably controlled fashion. Growth is great, but growth without profit I'm not really interested in. So the top line doesn't really matter as much as the bottom line does. Because ultimately, as the entrepreneur, that's what I'm here for. I'm here for the pay date.

So the plan is to grow the business 20 percent a year, to start an effective marketing program, which we actually started about 18 months ago. We started promoting the business in non-traditional ways, at least for companies that provide services like ours. Now we run radio advertising on a regular basis. We're on the radio in the major New York market, eight to ten times a day, 200 days of the year, promoting the business. So the objective is to generate a buzz about the company. There are a lot of small players in our space. We want to become *the* brand. We want to brand our name so that when clients or prospective clients think about using technology, we want them to think about us, even if it's not today, even if they don't need it for a year or two, because the projects that we get involved in, companies don't always do every year, they do every ten years, but we're just trying to make the impression. So we are going to grow the business by branding it and having a great roster of satisfied clients that can develop case studies so that we can be the go-to company.

Q: So what's your ultimate goal: to be a 50-million-dollar company?

A: You know, I'm 52 years old. At 20 percent a year I don't think I am going to see 50 million, but certainly the goal over the next couple of years is 20 percent a year. I hope to be done by the age of 60, 62—10 years from now. Not done—just done in that I want to have ensured that I set up a plan so the business survives me. It can't just be about me, because if I'm done in 10 years, the 70 people that I have employed at the time, what are they going to do? Where are they going to go? I have a deep sense of responsibility to them and I want to make sure that there is a succession plan in place.

That's what I'm going to do over the next 10 years. Grow it 20 percent a year and ensure that when I'm ready to be done, the business continues to live on.

Advice For New Entrepreneurs

Q: What advice would you give to young persons or start-up entrepreneurs?

A: If you've got a great idea, prove it. Prove it by building a plan—a business plan, a financial plan—that works. And once you've built it and you can put it on paper, then just go for it. Take the risk. The risk is worth it, because the rewards of entrepreneurship are enormous as opposed to continuing to work for somebody. There's nothing like being your own boss. There's nothing like calling the shots. There's a lot of headaches that go along with calling the shots, but at the end of the day, when you get to make the calls, when you get to determine when you stop and when you start, what direction to take, and you get to see that, it's very gratifying.

So take the shot. But make sure you are a realist. Your eyes are open. You have properly financed the venture, because the biggest problem, most of the businesses I see that have failed, is that they underestimated the initial capital requirements, and that they were going along a path and they just ran out of money. And if they'd had that cushion, that extra money to get them through the road they were going through, they probably could have built something substantial, but they didn't. They just didn't have enough capital to start the business. So you really have to make sure that your capital basis is sufficient and that your plan works. Put it down on paper. Understand: What does it mean? What does the idea mean? An idea is not enough. The idea has got to be supported with sound financial objectives. What are the objectives? Write them down. And then take the risk.

Q: The last time I was here you mentioned your nephew who is dyslexic, has learning disabilities, etc. Research shows that a lot of entrepreneurs—including many of my clients—tend to be not that educated. I have one guy who has an eighth or ninth grade education. So a lot of these people don't know financing. They don't have your background. So if they don't have that, how do they get it?

A: Well, that's a great thing. I would think that they would need to find a mentor, somebody…One of the things that I have learned is that you don't have to reinvent the wheel, you just find somebody else who has done it, and talk to them. Understand what they've done; copy what they've done in fact. You don't have to reinvent the wheel. So go out and find a mentor, find someone that has done it before. I can't tell you that I know where to find those people, but they exist. There are organizations, retired executives that are more than willing to get involved with entrepreneurs. They are looking for that. The retired executives are looking for an opportunity to help a business get off the ground.

You think about somebody who has been successful, has done something, an entrepreneur, an executive, who has reached retirement age. They're not done. There is plenty of vitality. Find that mentor. Find someone who can give you that, and then you don't have to have a great education. I didn't have a great education. I went to Brooklyn College. I went to Canarsie High School. I was an average student. I just had a desire to be successful. I wanted to be my own boss. I wanted to make a lot of money. And I wanted to make a difference. I wanted to make a difference and I put all that to work.

Running a business is no different than balancing a checkbook. If you can balance your checkbook, and you can understand how much you are getting, this is how much I am putting out, then you can understand the necessities of managing your expenses, understanding your costs, and then it's a matter of finding a client base and determining what they need and then filling that need. Filling that need with intensity because it's all about customers. All about clients. If your clients or customers aren't happy, just go home, no matter how good the product is. Whether it's a fabric design or the latest and greatest technology or decorating service, whatever it is. It doesn't make a difference how good it is. Are your clients satisfied? Do they feel like they are getting value?

So find that person who has been there, done it before, or even just read a book; frankly, just read a book, a simple book. There's a series of books that start out with *One Minute Manager*—a series of books that are very small, they are like 40, 50 pages, very easy English. So read a book [like that], and look at the people who have succeeded before, and just copy what they've done. That's what I've done and it has made a big difference for me.

Q: One more question before we finish. Maybe this doesn't apply so much to your company, but what are your thoughts on this whole threat of offshore technology? Your company seems to be in a market that you are not so threatened by your work being sent to India, China, or other places, but how do you evaluate that as a trend—more and more of the American technology and services being sent overseas?

A: We see a lot of that in the large companies where they can afford to go out and open up branch offices and manage an Indian or a Chinese office where they can outsource their work. Our business is personal service, so you can't outsource personal service. You can't outsource the ability to go out and reach and touch and consult with somebody knee to knee. So we don't really concern ourselves with that. We see it certainly as a growing trend. I believe it is a trend that will keep growing for a period of time, but there will be a backlash. And we've gotten involved in many outsource projects where we do Web developments, specifically on an outsource basis. To us as the person between the outsource people overseas and the client, the amount of management we have to do between the client and outsource company almost absorbs all of the rate differential that you achieve by going offshore with the work. So we found it's not a very effective model. Our cost structure might be a little bit higher but ultimately the management and the control is what ensures the quality of the project we do, so going offshore is never really an option. But there will be a backlash at some point. It will have to come back. There will be level of dissatisfaction with the clients. The clients will not be happy about the fact that they don't have the people they need to get to readily available to them, and there will be a return of more of that work coming back to America. I'm positive—because ultimately, the clients are not satisfied.

Those that I work with, the experiences I have as a consumer of consulting services from other technology companies, is horrible. So I look for alternatives where I can get a voice on the phone that I know will be able to help me in a reasonable amount of time without having to cross the language barrier.

Q: Well I want to thank you for the interview. It was very positive.

SUMMARY

Bart Nachimow attributes his company's success to its solid financial foundation—the fact that he has a firm grasp of the numbers. While many entrepreneurs don't have Bart's financial background, his story makes it clear that you *must* know—or learn—how to read profit and loss statements and perform cash flow analyses so you'll understand how your business makes its money. Simply put, your prices must be high enough to pay your expenses and still leave you with a profit.

Another key to Bart's success is his attitude toward his customers *and* his employees. He recognizes that customers are the lifeblood of any business, so he compensates his employees well and treats them like family, which makes them eager to provide exceptional service to their customers. His team is unfailingly loyal knowing that, even after Bart retires, the business will continue taking care of them, because he's put a succession plan in place that will secure the company's future.

CASE STUDY 3:
BEATRICE PIERCE

INTRODUCTION

Beatrice Pierce is the principal of Vento Corporation, which wholly owns Vespa Cibobuono, a successful Italian restaurant. Vespa Cibobuono is a 15-year-old business specializing in authentic Italian cooking and generates revenue between $1.5–$2 million annually. Originally founded by Beatrice Pierce and a partner in New York City, the restaurant began operation in Manhattan and is presently located in Great Neck, Long Island.

Initially, Ms. Pierce worked two jobs to financially stabilize the restaurant. After discovering that the partner was stealing money and embezzling company funds, Ms. Pierce negotiated a buyout to dissolve their existing partnership, which allowed her to continue operating at the current Northern Boulevard location. The restaurant's current patronage is working professionals whose median annual income is at or above $80,000. Over the past several years, the market has expanded considerably; now there is a strong family orientation of local residents and local businesspeople.

THE INTERVIEW

Background/History

Q: The first question I have for you is: Does your family have a history of entrepreneurship?
   A: No.

Q: How did you become an entrepreneur? What led you to this?

A: It's funny, now, you are using the word entrepreneur—it almost sounds like a foreign word to me because I don't think of myself as one. And I never did until you mentioned it to me just now. It was almost by chance—maybe chance isn't the right word—but it was by accident I would say. I was dating somebody who was already in the restaurant business. We had been dating for about a year or so when an opportunity came up in the city on Second Avenue to purchase this one tiny little restaurant, and he knew that more than one person was needed to work it. The only experience I had before that was the fact that in college everyone works in restaurants or in bars and so I ended up saying, "OK, let's try it."

We did talk about it because we were both going to be doing it—he'd only worked as managers in restaurants and I'd only done it in college—so the one thing that I did get from my family, even though nobody had a business background, was the strong work ethic. If you want something, you have to work. So I said OK. I knew it would be a lot of work, but at the same time, I had my other job, which made it a lot harder for me. So that's how it kind of got started. I knew someone—I was going out with somebody who was in the business, and then I just said, I'll try that also. And then one thing led to another. And a year later we opened up a second one.

Q: After you did it, did you get any support from your family at all?

A: Actually, no, they're a little more on the negative side. They said—they knew it was very hard. Anyone not even in the restaurant business would always say it was the hardest business to be in. And what they see is the hours, when people are always here late at night, working seven days a week, or six days a week, and they see those hours. My mother just kept on saying to me, "Just make sure you keep your day job." And I actually did keep my day job for seven years!

My parents were more excited because of the thought of their daughter owns a restaurant, that kind of thing. But on my end, I was thinking, "Oh my God, it is so much work." It's not glamorous because you are constantly working. You're up until three o'clock in the morning sorting out invoices, making sure you are paying the people because that's what you have to do. The only good part was somewhere towards the end of the night, I got to sit down and eat and drink, but then come nine o'clock, I had to be at work at my day job and then I'd do the same thing all over again at night.

Financing the Start-Up

Q: The reason I ask that question is because in books about other businesspeople, particularly the Harvard graduates, the Yale graduates, it always shows that at some point in their life their families stepped in and invested in their business, gave them seed money.

A: Oh, no. I've learned to save and not spend because once I took on that responsibility, I knew I was responsible for paying all the bills, all the utility bills, all the rents, all the taxes. And I grew up never asking—we weren't allowed to ask for anything because my parents had nothing. Because my father worked three jobs when we were really little. Because they had no money. My mother also worked. So as I said, we just worked. I didn't even think to ask for a loan or anything like that. I wouldn't do that. For one thing, I don't like paying back. I don't want to have to pay back somebody.

Q: So the way you financed it was to work not only one job, but two—you kept putting money into the business?

A: Right. I kept my day job and I did that for the first seven, eight years of the business. All that money was going into a joint account that my partner and I had, and then I also did freelance work. So whenever I could fit in some extra freelance work, because my trade is really graphic designer, I did freelance work to earn extra money. So mind you, once we opened up the first restaurant, then the second restaurant, I kept my day job only because that was who was paying my health insurance. Because at that point we couldn't afford to give ourselves a salary and we couldn't afford health insurance. So at least I had health insurance. And we thought if anything were to happen to us, at least I have my day job that could fill us in. Because we hear the stories of all the other restaurants, within two years you go under, there's a lot of money lost. So that's why we were afraid and we said, OK, it's better that at least one of us has a day job, and that was paying the things that we couldn't afford to pay somebody.

Q: As I recall, you mentioned you were in advertising or something?

A: Yes, and that made it easier for me too.

Q: How was that? How did that make it easier?

A: Well, it made it easier because, during my lunch hours, I had all the contacts when I needed my menus printed, when I needed my checks printed. If I wanted to do a little ad, I actually did it in the office. I did it on my lunch hour, or I snuck it in when I could if we were slow in the office. I snuck in doing all the—I actually did a lot of phone calls there because if no one could reach anyone in the restaurant, they knew they could always get me during the day. So all the accountants, or the lawyers, or the meat guy, they would call me up during the day and I was actually—I shouldn't have been doing it but I was actually doing some of the restaurant work as I was working. You're not supposed to, but that was what I was doing, and because I was able to still do my job, no one really said anything. They kind of knew my situation. So actually they were very, very good about it.

> Don't quit your day job—at least until you
> know the business can survive.

Q: So you just stumbled into a restaurant. One of my questions is why did you choose the restaurant? That's one of the hardest things to do.

A: My partner, the guy I was seeing and was living with at the time, if he happened to be owning shoes and said that [about going into business together], maybe it would have been a shoe business. Do you know what I'm saying? It just happened. I said, OK, let me try it. I'm a gambler. Well, not that kind of a gambler. But I'll try it. What's the worst that could happen?

I always say to everybody, I would feel worse about myself if I didn't try, than just be afraid. I would rather try and fail than not try at all. And that's how it kind of led into it, only because of my, I should say, ex-partner, that's a whole other story—

Q: I'll get into that in a minute.

A: I'll just say my ex-partner.

Q: When you opened the restaurant it was ten, eleven years ago?

A: No, fifteen.

Partnership Problems

Q: Let's go to the issue of your partner. As you told me before, you found your partner was embezzling funds, stealing money. How did you negotiate your way out of that arrangement? What did you do? I think there is a real lesson here.

A: The one thing I did learn is that—this actually did teach me a lot of things and I'm still learning stuff, but now what has happened is: I don't get surprised at anything anymore. I'm not surprised anymore about anything that comes to me. I do get disappointed at certain things, but I'm not really surprised.

What I've learned, for one thing, is definitely have a good accountant, and have a good lawyer. And besides that, have a contract—have a contract between two people.

Q: So you and your partner had a contract?

A: No, we didn't have a contract. Because when you are living with some-body, you think you are going to marry the person; you are not thinking any-thing is going to happen. You think, "It's all fine." And I was young—I was in my 20s and felt like doing all this kind of stuff and it was exciting, and how cool. It's a lot of work, but it's kind of cool, you know, that kind of a thing. And I didn't have a contract. Both our names were equally on the corporation, the checks, everything. We were both responsible. The liquor license has both our names on there.

What ended up happening after so many years, I learned more about the way of certain people. And his way was to believe—probably because I'm a female—that he had the right to do whatever he wanted to do. So I found out that he was taking money out of the account, but right in front of me. I would say to him, "You can't be writing a check for five thousand dollars. We have sales tax to pay." That's what I learned from my parents. If you have bills, you have to pay them. If somebody else doesn't pay me, I am still responsible for those bills. And that is what I was thinking. I was thinking more business. And I'm not a businessperson because my brain doesn't go that way—I'm more of an artist. To this day, I hate paperwork, to this day. And that's where the argument started.

He became so chauvinistic, in a sense, because he thought I should be doing everything he wanted to do, but it was hard because I felt like, "Well, I am still responsible. I still own half of this, and I am responsible for the bills. So I can't be doing that."

So that took about a year or so, and I saw that maybe I should have had a con-tract, because by then, you hear about the stories. But this is maybe eight years into the two restaurants, so, then, I hear of stories and people saying to me, "Well, you don't have a contract," this kind of stuff.

It's like a prenup I guess. You have certain things you have to fill out. And I said no. And then one thing led to another and he got a lawyer and I got a lawyer because I didn't want to come here one day and find my account empty. And the last thing that actually did it to me was one day I was going to make a cash deposit into the joint business account, and every time I made a cash deposit, I'd ask him, you know, what's the balance. And all of a sudden, the balance went from $150,000 down to $17,000! And that's like maybe after eight years of sav-ing money!

My whole insides fell out. I didn't think it was possible. That's another lesson I learned. Even though two people don't have a contract, either one of us could sign a check, but I thought, how can they allow someone to take out that much money, because if I were to put $15,000 into the bank, I have to fill out all these forms. It's the craziest thing. Anything under 10 you don't have to fill out any forms. Anything over 10 I think it is, over 9, you have to fill out these forms. So why would I think that someone would be allowed to take out $130,000?

I waited two weeks to see if he would do something crazy to put the money back in the account, but he never did, so I had to confront him and that was the end of the story. I got my lawyer. I had to sue him. I had to sue him! That money I never got back. But I sued him to get out of the restaurant. He walked away and we separated the two restaurants, because they were both ours. He kept the one in the city and I kept the one out here. Even then we had contracts saying that if anything happened up to a certain date, you know, if someone came to sue me and it was something that involved either restaurant, we were both responsible for it. And even then, I should have had other papers signed because we had a verbal agreement that if he were ever to sell that restaurant, he would ask me first. And I had the same thing here. If I ever wanted to sell out, just out of respect, we still both started it. He sold it to somebody else in the city.

> *Get it in writing.* Partnership agreements,
> service contracts, rights of first refusal—
> without a paper trail you have no proof.

Q: You didn't gain from the association. You just let him walk away with the restaurant.

A: Because it was worth it for me. In a sense, I consider myself a bad businessperson because I'm not into the money part of it. That's why I hate the paperwork end of it. I just want to be able to run the business, to have the people working here be very happy. I always give more to the people working here than I do myself, because it makes it better for me. It makes it easier for me to come in and do whatever I am going to do, or not come in because I know they can take care of it because they are happy being here.

I couldn't have my ex-partner over my head, always taking money out and doing things and never knowing what he's doing, just never knowing. And he became very crazy. One day he even threatened the restaurant, threatened to come in and spray paint everything. He would take out cases of wine, you know what I mean, and I'm the one paying for this. So I couldn't handle that. It became a very involved thing with him—it wasn't easy. It took a long time for the process to happen, for me to actually sue him, and for me to get out.

And the sad part of that is, with the money he took out of the account, he was able to buy himself an apartment building in Astoria. Once he had that apartment building, then he was able to take out equity and buy himself another restaurant down in the Carolinas. That restaurant led him to buy another restaurant in the Carolinas, and it was all from the money he stole out of our joint account.

I think he is doing OK, but you know what, for me, he is a very unhappy person. He thought that, because he had three restaurants and an apartment building, and then he also had an apartment in the city, he was going to be making all this money. What was happening was he couldn't be in all the places at the same time, and when one place was going under, he had to be there, so when he was at that place, the other place was going under because of the way he was running it. He just wasn't—it's just the way he is. And it's just his personality. He is who he is, and you know, I'll talk to him to this day, because he is who he is. I just learned my lesson not to be attached to him.

Managing the Business

Q: When you first started, when you were a graphic artist, a creative-minded person, did you start off with a formalized business plan that you wrote up on paper? Tell us how you started.

A: No. The restaurant in the city had only 40 seats, and I just knew from growing up, you buy something, you pay something. So when I got all my bills at the end of the month, I had to add them all up, and I had to pay them. I was working for the floor also. I was like the waiter. I was doing the floor and then my partner at the time was sometimes in the kitchen or he would be out on the floor also. We did what we needed to do. I didn't have a business plan though—I realized from just doing what I thought was common sense. I was thinking more common sense. You know, I have to get the people to come in so I can pay bills, because it was just the two of us. Maybe it was a little easier at the beginning because it was only 40 seats. So it wasn't like this big restaurant. But I learned you have to be really organized, and then once you are really organized, it makes a lot of things a lot easier to do. And then from that, from being organized, you have to write lists out, what needs to get done, what doesn't get done. I kind of learned that when I worked in the graphic supply business, the advertising agency.

There was a girl who worked there that was very strict with us because she was the creative director. We made fun of that—the fact that she was so strict. Every Monday, we had a list and we all had to have a meeting to see what was on that list and which job we were going to do, and once we were finished, we crossed them out. But you know what, all the fun that we made of her, it was one lesson that I really learned. I make myself a list.

I have to organize myself: what has to get done, whether it's talking to an accountant, how to handle certain taxes, what happens when the health department walks in. I just learned it. I learned it as I was going along and I didn't think about it as doing certain plans. I was just doing stuff in my head or writing down my list, not knowing I was organizing myself, just to make it easier for me, because once you see it on paper, you really don't forget it. And it's a really good feeling when you can cross things off. I was adding stuff, but at least you are still always crossing things off. So in that sense I can't say I didn't really have a professional business plan, but I just knew what had to get done. I just worked off of common sense at the beginning.

I would imagine people needing a business plan if they didn't have the opportunity that came to us. The people who owned the restaurant knew us from having dinner there and they offered to sell it to us, so the opportunity just came to us. I guess if I didn't have the opportunity at all and I just decided I wanted to be in any kind of business, then I would need a plan. I would have to prove to the person that I could do it, or prove to the bank that I could do it.

Q: The reason I ask that question is because business books tend to show that people who went through the big universities spent months on their business plans, and my argument is that, particularly for the people who are bootstrap entrepreneurs, they learn by doing. They don't have the formalized plan; it's common sense, as you say.

A: It's just common sense.

Q: Trial and error.

A: Yes, just basically a lot of common sense. And I also ask a lot of questions of people. I ask everybody questions. That's how I learn. I just don't go in there thinking I could do it on my own.

Q: How did you learn to manage those business skills? How did you develop an understanding of, for example, what the IRS requires, and the credit? I know you said you have a good accountant, but how did you train yourself for that?

A: Well, you know, it was actually very difficult. But, like I said, I ended up being the one responsible for all the bills. And that's the biggest part that no one ever really sees. No one ever sees in the restaurant business what you do behind the dining room floor, so to speak. Because I was the one responsible, I had to make sure that at the end of every month, I looked at all my stuff, and especially when it came to the IRS. I learned that through a bad lesson with my ex-partner, and I also had accountants who I later realized were bad, but I didn't know that at the time. When you are dealing with the same people and nothing is going wrong and everything is OK, you don't think about it.

One day I had the IRS say they were going to audit me—I owed them a lot of money because my original accountants never really filed correctly. But I was filing the same way every year, so I didn't know I was doing anything wrong. My accountants didn't catch anything that was being done at their end until one day when I was caught. Then they basically said, "Oops, I guess we did make a mistake."

The IRS ended up going back seven years and it was a big mess. Because of that, I realized that you get what you pay for because my accountants were like dead cheap a month, but like I said, I didn't know. It was my first business, so I thought maybe paying $250 a month for an accountant for two businesses, for one business, is OK. I didn't know maybe it should have been $400 or so a month, because they would have caught that mistake that happened with the IRS.

Even though my ex-partner and I were both responsible according to the contract we had when we separated the two businesses—this happened when he was still here—but because of that one mistake, I became the one responsible for that mistake. But to try and catch someone to make them pay, it took me four years after that—at least four years. By then, I was the one still responsible for paying an $80,000 debt. So what ended up happening was that after taking that many years trying to do that, when it came time to settle, he ended up settling for less. But by that point, I just wanted to be done and over it. I like to get rid of big major things off my head. That was a big thing. I was suing him for the money he owed me.

Q: So how did you get on top of the situation—to say, "Now I know how to manage it"? What did you do?

A: Well, I got myself a lawyer and I made him responsible because I learned—it took me quite a few years to learn—how to delegate. So I had to delegate the responsibility. At first, you want to do everything yourself, the way you want it done, because then it gets done the right way, but then I had to learn that you have to step back and delegate because there is no way you can do everything. And even though someone doesn't do it exactly the way you might do it, for me, as soon as you step foot into the restaurant, if it looks like it's OK, then that's fine for me. All those little things I can fix as I go along. So I had to learn…It took me a long time, but I got a bookkeeper. At the time, I was doing it myself. The first two years I was doing everything myself in both places, plus working the day job.

I figured it was a way of saving money. But when it got to be too much, I said, "Let me just get a bookkeeper."

At that time my mother needed a job. My partner said, "Why don't you hire your mother? She isn't going to steal from you." So I said OK. She was glad to be working here, and I didn't think anything of it. I said, "Fine, get rid of all that paperwork." I showed her how I wanted it done and she just started doing it.

We were in maybe our second year of business when she started working here—she was with me for six or seven years, but after so many years, I had to fire her. It took me quite a few years to do that—if she wasn't my mother I would have fired her four years earlier. But everybody around me was saying, "But she's your mother, she's your mother, don't worry about it, she's your mother."

What are you going to do? She would always come in late, leave early, do all her personal work instead of doing the restaurant work, on the phone all the time with her friends for hours. And then I would get so frustrated, so annoyed at her. One time she came to work on the day that I am normally not here during the day, and I happened to pull up, because I always come in randomly whenever I happen to pull up, and I see her getting out of her car in the parking lot. And by this time she is already over an hour late getting there. And mind you, she only has to be here from eleven to six. She doesn't work eight hours. She picked her own hours, from 11 o'clock to 6 o'clock. She came at 12 o'clock, and she says she was stuck in traffic. And I just closed my eyes. I said, "Ma, you still have the pedicure paper wrapped around your toes." I said, "You had your nails done." You know what I mean? And that became the biggest joke because she was always giving me an excuse. She wanted to leave early because she wanted to go food shopping. Or she wanted to leave early because she wanted to see her girlfriends. I said, "You can't do that." I was giving her a good salary. She was taking home five hundred a week. I'm fair, but once you start taking advantage of me, that's where I draw the line.

> Love family and friends, but don't necessarily
> hire them. Develop a contract for people
> working with you, and make sure you spell out
> their duties and responsibilities.

Q: How important was it for you to develop a team, and how did you develop that team?

A: By practice…but that's not really the right word because we did have other people who came in here to work and they didn't work out, so of course they left, but once you got to see someone's personality and that personality worked with you, and it happened to work with the people who are here, then you kept that person. If a new person came in and they liked even the way we all are, then they stayed because it was comfortable for them. Same thing with my chef. My chef is wonderful. His name is Alberto Siabache. And he was here—actually he was here when the restaurant in the city opened up. And when this one opened up, we had to separate the two chefs so one stayed here and one stayed there. So Alberto stayed here because he was good and it was comfortable for him. Also, I'm not strict. When my ex-partner was here, it was very difficult for them because he would always—I am not somebody who yells and screams and I find a lot of Italians and a lot of hot-tempered people would do that. They go in there yelling and screaming…

They also see that whatever I ask of them, I'll do myself. I don't expect them to clean a dish off my table after I've eaten if I don't do it myself. I'm not like that. I'll help the guy in the kitchen clean if he needs help cleaning. So they see that of me—that I am willing. I do for them and they do for me, and it becomes a big circle. To me, it's like a family. It has to be like a family. They are working. They are the ones who are really doing all the hard work.

Q: What exactly do you do? Do you just kind of oversee everything because the rest of them tend to run the restaurant?

A: The guy in the kitchen, the chef runs the kitchen and then we all do certain things with the ordering. We know the vegetable purveyor. He knows us. And we know our fish guy. Everybody knows all of us. And so it's between Alberto, myself, and the manager, who is my right hand man, Francesco. All of us do some kind of ordering.

Also, now, because my mother is not here anymore, I'm back to doing all the paperwork. So that is taking a good part of my time. I'm doing research—trying to find out about doing a commercial maybe; trying to get loans for the corner piece of property—so that is taking a long time. It's very involved. And a lot of stuff now I either do out of my little office in my apartment because I have a computer, my little fax machine, I do from the apartment, or I have the office downstairs in the basement here. So, like I said, I'm here non-stop Friday, Saturday, and Sunday. So I can put in 40 hours in three days. And during the beginning of the week, I either work on the floor or I come in and I go. If I know that everything is OK, then I can leave and I can do something else—go pick up supplies, stuff like that.

Overcoming Obstacles

Q: What do you think are the biggest mistakes you made in the last 15 years, and how did you recover from those mistakes?

A: Not having a contract with my partner. That was the biggest one, because even though we were still 50-50, I had to end up paying him $75,000, just to be done with it. I actually paid him off just to be out of here. And at that time, also the biggest mistake was not researching lawyers. Because the lawyer I had at that time, after I signed that agreement, he actually said to me, "You know what, you never should have paid that." And I looked at him and said, "What the f***!" I said, "That's what you're for." So when he told me I never should have paid that $75,000, that's when I got rid of the lawyer.

At that point I had to pay it, so in a sense I had to take out a loan to pay him the $75,000. Two years after that, I found that I owed all that back tax money. My biggest thing was not having a contract with my partner. No matter who you are—I tell that to people to this day: I don't care if it's your brother, your mother, I don't care who it is—you have a contract. Everything is on paper. That way there are no questions, no problems. That was my biggest mistake.

Q: Could you describe it in personal terms? When you were going through this big mistake, were you depressed, suicidal? I know you have a happy personality.

A: No. I had to look at it as my fault. Not that it was my fault that I should have known better, but I didn't know any better. That also was my fault. Maybe I didn't do enough research when I—it's like anything else, when people get married, they don't plan on getting divorced. So it's the same thing; it's really the same thing.

I just said, "Oh my God, I have to pay all this money. What am I going to do?" So I ended up thinking, I just had to work harder, and I didn't spend anything. I didn't waste anything, I should say. And because it was just me, now it was only me, and solely me doing everything, I just had to…I couldn't blame anybody else but myself.

And I'm someone who has to look forward. I can't look behind. I can only look forward and say, OK, it became so bad that it was better struggling for quite a few years than to have him still be a partner. So to me it was more worth it to struggle than to have him as a partner. What I did learn was to have a contract with everyone. I don't care who it is.

Q: So, why a high-end Italian restaurant? It's hard enough to do a restaurant—you have a high-end restaurant.

A: Actually, it's not quite high end. To me, it's more in the middle. It just became what it was, from the type of food that we were selling the very first year…It kind of evolved in itself. And people liked what we had. We're not fancy. It's just good honest Italian food, and it's really good.

Looking Toward the Future

Q: You are still a young woman. What are your future goals and challenges? What lies ahead for you?

A: Challenges is a good word. Because I do like a challenge, and I think that's what helped me through all of this, because I am sure a lot of people thought I wasn't going to do it, and it's more so even when you are a female, trying to get things done. But I just overlooked that. And I can't let that bother me because I know what I have to do and I know where I have to be to pay for certain things, and right now that place is running good and I have a wonderful manager. That's what got me to the corner piece of property. So that's my next challenge. I want to do a little gourmet shop now. It's a business I must learn; I already took a class in the city and I'll take more classes. I'm going to the food shows, and the gourmet specialty shop shows so I can learn how to do that stuff. So I know at least, I am taking my time and I will learn how to do that.

Q: One of the people I interviewed was a high school dropout who built a successful trucking company; then at the age of 60, he decided the future of the world is China, so he sold his trucking company and opened up an airfreight company. Since you seem to be an adventurous person, could you see yourself just going out of the box and doing something like that?

A: If I knew of an opportunity, like I wouldn't know anything about that…Yeah, I think I would. It's exciting. How can it not be exciting? How can you not try?

The one thing I do have going for me—it depends on how you look at it—I am not married and I have no kids, so I don't have to worry about that responsibility. That's why really it's easier for me to say I will take that chance because I don't have to worry about putting somebody through school. So in that sense it is easier for me. I don't have that responsibility. I have the restaurant as a responsibility, but I don't have that as a responsibility. It is a lot easier for me to say, yeah, maybe I'll try that. In a different country, wow!

Q: Do you think women have more problems in business? Do you think it is harder for women in business?

A: Yes. On the whole, yes.

Q: How?

A: Because to this day, when I have the responsibility of having to meet someone, or do something, or get something, I have to make sure that I do it and I am exactly on time. I don't want someone to say, "Look at her, she thinks she can do what a typical female does." I don't want that. What I find more often than not is that it's the men who are always late, the men who don't produce what they say they are going to produce, and I can't say it's just the men, I think it's because it's in the business. There's just more men. And that's why.

But I find when I have to be—even at a lawyer, I am there exactly on time. He might be there forty minutes late and no one thinks to give me a phone call and say they're going to be late. And that's what bothers me sometimes. I find that I have to make sure that I'm there when I am supposed to be there, and most men don't take me seriously. They just think because I am always smiling and I am enjoying it so much—because I actually don't think of it as work, it's just what you have to do—they don't think I'm serious. And that could be my problem.

I'm not stricter. Maybe I don't dress the part. That's just who I am, so this is who I am. I am not changing. So I have to keep on calling up and calling up—that's why Francesco has ended up being my right-hand man—because he deals with certain people that would rather deal with him. And after all these years, I don't want to be saying, "You only have to deal with me." So I say, "You know what, you want to talk to the wine guy, you talk to the wine guy because you're Italian, they're Italian"—it just makes it easier.

I found that even when I tried talking about loans or talking to contractors, electricians, they just talk and talk and think I don't know what I am doing and they never come back. So I am calling up and calling up and I'm like, don't these people want the job? Don't they want to work? They're in business. Don't they want to have this job? Even to do the contract, when I did the renovation in here, you have no idea what I went through to get the renovation done. I would have people come in to give me their estimates, tell them what I wanted, how much it would cost. It took me months before someone thought I was serious. So even when I talk to other people, other females, they just say, it is a lot harder. But a lot of times you are in business with someone else who can take care of it.

So when you are doing it by yourself, you have to kind of overcome that. I said, I'll just keep on pushing forward. I just push forward. And I don't let that bother me. But if you gave me the question yes or no, yes, I am going to say it is harder for females. You have to prove yourself more. For some reason they don't think you can do it. And to this day I still think—my girlfriend who has two kids, I think she has a harder job. I think it is harder to be 24/7 with kids than it is with the business. That's a harder job. That's why I don't want to do it.

Q: I know you told me that some of your employees have been with you for 13 years. Do you have any kind of retirement planning assistance?

A: This is what I did with my manager—I have a contract with my manager because I learned to have a contract—he gets so much money of the profits, so in a sense, that's the thing for him. He gets *x* amount of money based on the profits of the business. He gets his manager's salary and he gets a percentage of the profits. Also, if the place increases over a certain amount—like we have a steady increase, or if for whatever reason, it really jumped up high, he gets an additional bonus for the difference of that increase. Also, if the business is ever sold, I am giving him a cut of the business, and that's a lot. And also every month I give him a couple of hundred towards his medical. So that's his incentive. He does pretty well.

I have a waiter who has also been here for 11 years. I sponsored him. He has his green card, but you know what, like I said, it's like we all grew up together really, they make good money here, so like anything else, I'm sure they could make better money someplace else, even if it's the same, if this place were horrible, then they would go. But you know, we all have a good time because I'm not a hard person; I just think you should have a good time as you are working.

Q: I always thought you were born in the wrong era. You should have been a hippie back in the '60s.

A: I should be. People always call me a gypsy. But you should have a good time. You have to have a good time when you are working. You have to enjoy coming in the door. You might not enjoy dusting and cleaning, I mean, who does? I don't even like doing that. But the actual total, the whole job, you have to enjoy it so it comes across to the people. And occasionally people do change, but I do see the same people here. They want to see the same faces, which makes it nice, which makes it easier for me. So that's what I'm saying. It makes it easier for me because then I can step back further and do other stuff, and I'm giving more to them so they are happy doing what they are doing. So it's good.

Advice For New Entrepreneurs

Q: Although you are still a young person, what advice would you give to someone who wanted to start up a business, to enter a business? Based on what you know now, what advice would you give them?

A: I would say, go ahead, go for it, but do all your research first, to have some of your own personal money to back things up. For me, I was doing two jobs at the same time. That was my way of backing this up. I was still getting a paycheck at my day job and I was doing freelance work still, so that was my backing up. I didn't have money in the bank just to put forward, so in a sense that was how I was backing it up.

I would say, do a lot of research, organize your accounts and make sure there are good accountants, and ask people, even their clients, ask people about their accountants, ask people about their lawyers so you can pick a good lawyer for yourself and a good accountant for yourself. You need to have that. You need to start that first, because they are the ones who are going to guide you through everything. When you have a business, you are going to have to go to those two people for everything, from the business end of it, for everything.

And then just have a passion to do it and don't let anyone tell you that you can't do it. Try it—you just have to try it. You have to do that. I don't know how people don't want to try it. Unless they are too afraid, but then try something smaller so you can do it. Or go to someone who is doing something like what you are doing, or exactly what you are doing, and see how they did it. See if they can help you out. Or maybe they might have people that could also work with you, like their accountant or their lawyer.

So I would just say, if someone wants to go and do it, they need to have the passion to do it and be ready to make sacrifices if that's what it takes.

SUMMARY

Beatrice Pierce runs a highly profitable restaurant now, but in the beginning, her success and business survival hinged on learning what *not* to do. Her story emphasizes the importance of getting the right people in place to help you in the right way at the right time; accountants and lawyers, for example, should be hired to help you minimize your financial exposure.

Even when you're operating on a shoestring budget, you must plan and implement management strategies that make all parties involved in the business accountable. This includes having a partnership agreement with *anyone* you bring in as partner, as well as paying for professional help to make sure your finances are in good order. The IRS does not accept excuses. In order to succeed in business, you must educate yourself in the language of business to avoid costly mistakes that could prove financially fatal.

CASE STUDY 4:
PATRICK HEANEY

INTRODUCTION

Patrick Heaney is President of Republic Cargo Systems Inc. He has been in the transportation industry for over thirty years. Patrick, a high school drop out, purchased a truck after his discharge from the armed forces and started his business. He built a national trucking company with headquarters in New York and California. Approximately six years ago, Patrick decided that the future in the freight business was air transportation and he sold his trucking company.

As a startup, Patrick decided that Republic Cargo Systems should focus on transporting apparel from the Asian market. His company currently has offices in China and India. His list of clients includes Tommy Hilfiger, TJ Maxx, Liz Claiborne, and others. His office, with a staff of nine people, is located in the JFK airport vicinity.

The company is presently opening additional offices throughout China. In the past, Patrick received a certificate from the Harvard Business Department Entrepreneur Program. He also was honored with an outstanding achievement award from former President Ronald Reagan.

THE INTERVIEW

Background/History

Q: Thanks for the interview, Patrick. Since I know a little bit about you, let me ask you my first question: What inspired you to open a business after you got out of the Army?

A: Well, actually, probably from about the time I was ten years old, all I really wanted to do was be in my own business. Probably one of the most inspiring things for me was I really couldn't get a good job because I never completed a high school program, so in order to be able to create a lifestyle for myself and eventually my family, I felt the best way to do it would be in my own business.

Q: What was your mother's reaction when you told her you wanted to go into business, and did you get any support from your family to get started?

A: No, actually not. My parents are immigrants from Ireland and my mother kept saying, "Get a good job, work for the city. Get some security—a lifetime position." Something I wasn't interested in. I felt that you could always make a living if you wanted to work. This is America. If you want to work, there's plenty of jobs out there.

Financing/Managing the Business

Q: From what I've noticed about people who graduated from the big colleges, their families were generally very influential in giving them start-up money. With you, it was probably just the opposite.

A: My parents had nine children. My father was a longshoreman for 40 years, and whatever extra money I could spare I was always giving it all to my family.

Q: So how did you obtain your start-up funds?

A: Well, actually, I started with one truck. I was able to accumulate enough money to put a down payment on a truck which I think was about $800 for a $3000 piece of equipment, and that's how I got started.

Q: Why did you choose trucking?

A: Well, I drove a truck for 4-1/2 years for a big freight outfit in New York. And actually, why I started, was an opportunity presented itself to a good friend of mine who introduced me to a customer that needed to have their cargo removed on the piers of New York, so I decided to give it a shot.

Q: I remember once when you spoke at York College and someone asked you the question: "What kind of business plan did you have when you started?"

You probably don't remember this, but in response you pointed to your head and said, "My business plan was right here!" So maybe you could describe how you planned this out, what did you do to map out your start-up if not a business plan?

A: Well, actually, with no formal education, basically not understanding the true business process, I derived a plan practically on a step-by-step basis. My first truck kept me busy enough to get a second truck, and then a third one, and then a fourth one. And so on and so forth. I started in March 1968 with the one truck. By 1972 I had about 30 trucks and started a warehouse business, because I saw a need for it. Basically, how I derived the business plan was: I listened to my customers and I tried to fill the needs that they required. Just strictly doing trucking, and eventually customers said they needed places to store their goods, so I established a warehouse business.

Q: But you also mentioned one time that there was this organization on the docks that you went to and said, "I could do this better for you, let me move your cargo another way." So how did you gain a competitive edge?

A: Well, what happened, what launched my career was initially when I started it was what we called "break bulk"—there were no containers. And timing was good; it was just initially about '65 or '66 when a lot of major apparel manufacturers started to ship their production from the United States over to Asia. The cargo would arrive in basically smaller lots, so we would use smaller equipment. When I saw the volume start to increase I was probably one of the first trucking companies in New York to start using tractor-trailers on the New York waterfront, and volume went from picking up 50 cartons to picking up 50 trailer loads on a ship. And then by '73/'74, containerization started to come into full swing, probably about 1976. It was basically all containerized.

So, what I did was in December of 1968, six months after I initially started, I was introduced to a company called Holly Stores which was the ladies' apparel division of K-Mart, and as they grew and their demands kept increasing, I kept buying additional equipment, additional trucks, to service basically that customer. And because I was doing a lot of business for K-Mart at the time, a lot of importers that were really basically just starting out, that were selling K-Mart, looked to them for direction. Because of my relationship with K-Mart, they referred me to a lot of additional business, which kept allowing me to expand my companies from trucking companies into warehouse companies. Then, around 1977, American President Lines, who I was doing a lot of work for, asked me to joint venture with them and set up an ocean consolidation business in Asia for the apparel and retail industry, and that turned out to be a very successful program that I was involved with for almost 25 years.

> Visualize possible scenarios and assess
> opportunities. Work out the steps to achieve
> your goals and objectives.

Q: So you essentially went from local to national, right?

A: Local to international.

Q: But didn't you tell me one time that you were local, then you had an agency in California, that you were kind of shipping back and forth between New York and Bakersfield or some area like that?

A: Well, eventually what H&M, the company I initially started, evolved into was a company with about 23 operating divisions. We had, when I sold it in the year 2000, we had 600 trucks, 3-1/2 million square feet of warehousing and distribution space, seven rail terminals which we operated for various steamship companies, and an ocean consolidation business on partnership with APL in Asia, the American consolidation services.

Q: And how did you handle the business management in the beginning? What was your level of business expertise? I mean, when you start a business you have to do invoicing, you have to meet with the IRS, you have to read financial statements, how did you gain those skills?

A: Actually, it was kind of funny, when I sent my first invoice out to my customer, to my first customer's company called ES Novelty, I sent out about four or five invoices, so I could get paid, and again not having any formal education or understanding of bookkeeping or simple accounting practices, I remember the customer calling me and telling me, "I want to pay your invoices, but there are no invoice numbers." Actually, I didn't know what an invoice number was, so I said, "If you need a number, put one on there and just pay it."

So that was—I didn't understand what accounts receivable were, what accounts payable were. But I realized early on my shortcomings and managed to surround myself with people that had more academic training than I did, and were able to direct me in those various areas. My basic experience was just basically good common sense, a little bit mixed with a little bit of "street smarts" and a dire ambition to be successful.

Q: What about native intelligence? I know when people talk about you, they say, "Well, Patrick is a very smart man." So somewhere along the line you must have figured out all this stuff, how to do this by listening to your accountant, listening to your better half or something.

A: Well my accountants will give you guidance somewhat, what's a profit, what's a loss. Attorneys will give you counsel on what's right and what's wrong. What it really boils down to is just having enough sense to make correct decisions, when to open new operations, when to start new companies, when to get new business, when to hire additional personnel—operating personnel, sales personnel, administrative personnel. So, basically, kind of the guidance of common sense.

Q: At this point, Patrick, would you say that you can read financial statement balances and so forth as well as anybody right now?

A: Well, I'm self-educated, self-taught.

Q: How did you teach yourself this?

A: Kind of trial and error. Over the years I've had some pretty good Certified Public Accountants working for me as Chief Financial Officers, and we'd basically sit down with them and walk through different things. Once you have the basic formula, then it's just a matter of "Is the glass half full?" or "Is the glass half empty?" It depends which way you want to look at it. And not everything you want to see in a business is basically in a balance sheet. You have to look beyond that; you have to look at where are the synergies, where are the opportunities, where can businesses be built from, what can they be created from?

Q: Right. I don't know if you remember but you told me that when you first met your wife she was interested in doing the invoices, and you were interested in getting next to her.

A: Yeah, initially when we first started my wife would help me do the billing because she was a secretary and could type, and I was hand writing everything, and it became necessary to start typing the invoices when I started doing business with a lot of large corporations, and my wife was kind enough to come over to my apartment on Sundays and help me type up these different invoices.

Q: But invoicing wasn't on your mind all the time.

A: Yeah, that's true. That's what happens when you're young.

Lessons Learned

Q: So during that period, when you were building the trucking company, what were some of the big mistakes or basic lessons that you learned?

A: Well, I didn't actually make a lot of mistakes early on. I kept growing—kind of paid attention to what the big guys were doing. For instance, one of the best-run trucking companies in the United States is United Parcel Service. UPS uses a specific type of tractor called a "Mack" and actually I just went out and duplicated that. I bought all the same type of trucks. I said, "If it's good enough for them, it's good enough for me." I wouldn't say that I made too many mistakes, because I probably built one of the most successful companies in that business. If there probably were any shortfalls, off the top of my head, I really can't think of any.

Q: One time you said you "lost millions." What did you mean by that—was that from business errors?

A: Well, in business you have what you call inside forces and outside forces, outside forces being things that are beyond your control. I had 600 trucks—600 independent contractors. I owned the trailers; they owned the tractors. And in 1997/1998, I received a penalty from the Internal Revenue Service because the tax code said I owed them $13.5 million because I didn't pay the tax on what were independent contractors. The IRS was classifying them as employees, but we maintained they were independent contractors. And to get through that litigation was three and a half to four million dollars. We had some rather major difficulties with the bank at the time because we had to post a liability on our balance sheet. We had certified statements. Our banks canceled my line of credit. And I was able to get involved with a "work-out" situation with Chemical Bank that took me about a year and a half, but to satisfy the banks and satisfy my creditworthiness, I had to liquidate some of my assets and bring back the operations of then about a $90–$95-million-dollar company down to a $65-million-dollar company. And there was never a settlement reached with the IRS, they were never paid. What actually did happen was they just went away. And we never had a hearing on it, and I was one of probably 500 trucking companies in the United States that used independent contractors, but unfortunately myself and one other company in California were the only two people that were, you might say, were "put on the cross."

Q: So you went from $95 million to $65 million?

A: I liquidated; I sold off some of my assets, some of my warehouse companies, and was able to take the cash proceeds. I sold back my interest in the consolidation business in Asia, I sold my warehouse companies, and I was able to take that cash and completely remove all my financial issues. At the time I was strongly advised to file a Chapter 11 and it was just my own tenacity that wouldn't allow me to do that. I felt my reputation was worth a lot more than a few dollars that I had to pay. And again, it's what we call an outside force. As far as I'm concerned, I did nothing wrong, but I suffered a lot because of what the government decided to do.

Q: So, when you say "suffered"…

A: Financially.

Q: Now, I'm looking at the human side: Did you get depressed? Did you feel like giving up? Did you start drinking a little bit?

A: No, I never felt like giving up. And I never took to drink. It wasn't my style—I saw too much of that growing up.

Q: What I'm interested in is how you reacted?

A: Well, mostly it was a constant drain on me. I mean, here was a company I created from nothing and I saw outside forces driving it into the ground. And emotionally it was very disturbing. You have to have tenacity sometimes and the will to fight things that are, like I said, beyond your control. And you hang in tough and you get things done. You know, one thing I believe, one thing I strongly believe in, and I still do today, and I preach it to all my people, is that when you have a problem, 'fess up to it, don't try to dump it. Talk your problems through with the people you do business with, let them get a better understanding of what you're doing. Be up front and be honest, that's the best way to operate.

Q: During this period of stress, did your family step in and really take a role and help you get through this emotionally?

A: Well, emotionally I got complete support from my family, from both my wife and from my children. They were very understanding. My wife was completely understanding. I mean, my wife and I come from very humble beginnings, and we created a lifestyle that we never really anticipated. However, we were fortunate enough to be able to do it and we enjoyed it, and I wasn't about to give that up. So I got, I happen to have a wonderful marriage for 37 years, and my wife basically stood behind everything that I did. My sons at the time were too young to really understand it, but as they got older they did, and they always had—I have an extraordinary relationship with my three children.

Changing Things Up

Q: Was it that difficult period that led you to sell off your trucking operation and go into international freight?

A: Well, I had to make a decision. Here I had a very heavy asset-based company that required a lot of capital, warehouses, a lot of commitments. And I decided that I would stay in the airfreight business and dissolve myself of the capital-intensive business—stay in what we call a non-asset-based business, which worked extremely well for me and is getting better.

Q: What made you decide to take the plunge into China?

A: Well, I mean today everything you read is "China, China, China." I had lunch last week with a friend of mine that's looking to start a career and he asked me what I thought, what kind of a business did I think he should go into, and I said "I only got one word for you and that's 'China.' You're young enough, smart enough, go over there. Make a career." It's the land of opportunity.

I visited China the first time in 1980 and basically saw nothing, but I'd been traveling by that time in the Orient for three or four years, so I kind of understood that the work the Asians were doing was second to none; they would do anything to try to make something successful. Very hard-driving, very hard-working people. Felt it was the kind of people that I wanted to be involved with; saw that once China was able to relieve itself of some of their political restrictions that they would eventually become a major powerhouse. And that's exactly what's happening today. And my belief today, twenty years later, is they're just getting started.

> Free your mind and seize new opportunities. There
> are new markets to penetrate, constant change, and
> global experiences to take advantage of.

Q: What were your initial concrete steps to get started in China?

A: Well, we actually opened an office in Shanghai around 1979, 1980 with my ocean consolidation business. Now, with my airfreight company we have seven offices in seven major cities in China.

Q: China is becoming a manufacturing hub of the world.

A: Exactly.

Q: How did you find or develop local partners?

A: Well, I have a partner now in my company, Mr. Philip Woo, who we have been together now for about eight years. A very aggressive, young, hard-working, honest, very structured individual, and he's helped greatly in the success of the company. I handle the U.S. side of things, Philip handles the Asian side.

Q: How did you find him?

A: Actually, I was introduced to him through a good friend of mine. He was in a similar business and when we met we worked together on a couple of major projects and one day I asked him, I said, "Philip, you want to, you want to get married? You want to become my partner?" and we talked about it for about two months. At the end of the two months, he said, "Yes, let's do it." So that's how we became partners.

Q: And he's the only partner you have, or you have multiple partners?

A: No, he's my only partner. Well, last January 1st we made my son Brian the President of the company, and we gave him a 10% interest in the company.

Q: Earlier you mentioned the negative things about the government coming in on your trucking company. Internationally, have you found any governmental programs? Have you utilized any that would further your international business?

A: Not really. Basically our business is mainly wearing apparel, garments, footwear, accessories, merchandise dealt with in retail stores, so we don't really get involved with any type of government contracts or government situations. What help we do get from the government is, for instance, re-normalization of relationships with China. Now there's a very strong thought that Vietnam, which is one of our major offices, will become part of the World Trade Organization (WTO), because they were able to lift their restrictions against imported merchandise from the United States. Because of that fact, our Commerce Department has issued support for Vietnam's application to the WTO, which they said is going to happen this year, so that's going to open up more opportunities in China. Also, one of the other things the government did, as part of the negotiations, they had the Vietnamese government open up opportunities, foreign logistics companies operating within the country.

Q: So you know of all the hot spots, Vietnam, China, the real tough countries.

A: Yeah. Vietnam and China. Well, China's not so tough. It's very—Chinese people are very smart businesspeople. And not a difficult person to do business with—that's why they have expanded so well for the last twenty years.

Q: Over the next few years, how much revenue do you think you can generate with your Chinese business?

A: We could double, triple, or quadruple our business with China. Our market share is very insignificant. We're pretty sizable, but yet we have an insignificant market share. The market is so vast.

Q: So what will it take for you to—

A: Just continuing adding customers to the base area. Personnel that will be able to handle the business, both from an operations side and a sales side.

Q: So you've been doing this Chinese business about six years now, right?

A: Well, we've got our own offices in China for about six years but I've been involved with doing business in China since about 1980.

Q: Okay, so let me ask you this, then. For this new business, the international freight business, what are the valuable lessons that you learned so far from that business?

A: Well, I don't know if you want to call it a lesson, but just a matter of providing a first-class airfreight service for our customers to be sure that the cargo they entrust to us gets delivered on time, developing a reputation for building up an account base. One account tells another account tells another account, and you can go to your customers and use them for references on new sales opportunities, new customers.

Looking Toward The Future

Q: So, you're still a young man, Patrick. What are the future goals and challenges you see ahead of you? I don't think you're ever going to retire.

A: No, I have no desire to retire as long as I'm healthy. My goal now is to see this company double in size in the next three years. That's a 30% compounded increase each year, sales and revenue and profits. That's kind of very ambitious, but very attainable.

Q: And what are your personal goals—how would you like to see yourself? I know that's the business side, but what would you like to see?

A: It's like my wife says, "Patrick's happiest when he's working," so I'd like to see myself spending less time in the day-to-day operations and more time in overall planning of the company, what we should be doing next and where we should be going, what type of customers we should be talking to, and who we should be doing business with, and how to achieve that.

Q: More golf, more—

A: Golf is fun, but I can only play four or five months a year, so I enjoy that. Now that my third son is getting married, we're going to have the empty nest syndrome, so what I want to do with my wife—we're going to continue traveling, what we do enjoy is world travel. I'm not the type of guy that wants to park his ass down in Florida for six months a year, so basically I could travel all over the world and do business.

We have agencies in 18 countries in Asia, agencies in Africa, Madagascar, European agents, all types, so I'd like to spend more time developing those relationships and expanding that business.

Q: So for someone who started with nothing—a kid coming out of Brooklyn—I guess you could say that you created a generation of wealth for your family. It's no longer just Patrick here, it's Patrick's grandchildren and whoever that have a "head start," right?

A: Well, yeah, they're not going to have to start from the bottom of the ladder. I think, more importantly than establishing a generation of wealth is what I pride myself on, that I've been able to instill in my sons the importance of having a strong work ethic and very strong family values.

Q: I was reading an article about the NBA player, Shaq. He stated that his children and grandchildren will be taken care of for a long time. But I like what you said, in that you taught your sons how to work hard and how to achieve.

A: You don't do it by preaching, you do it by example. My oldest son Patrick chose not to be in this business and went into the construction business about four years ago. And now he's got his own offices, he's got 14 employees and he's building houses, doing commercial. He's got a nice business. It's fun for me to sit down with him every few months over at dinner, just the two of us, and discuss some of the pros and cons of what he's doing. So I have that kind of a relationship, which is nice. It's funny how a lot of different people say to me, "You really built a successful business, what do you consider the most successful part of it?" And I always say, "My family." I have a relationship with them—my three closest friends are my sons, and also my wife.

Q: I know you have a lovely family. I've met them.

A: Thank you.

Q: What about your retirement benefits for your employees? Have you—

A: One of the things I pride myself on is that in my business, I've always made sure that my employees are well taken care of. We have probably one of the best health care plans out there. It's expensive, but I have no problem paying. I also have a very good 401K plan with matching funds. I also have a very liberal vacation and personal day policy. My business is a service business. In order to operate a service business, you've got to have employees—you pay peanuts, you get monkeys. It's that simple.

Q: And your people tend to stay a long time with you, too.

A: Yeah, I've had truck drivers working with me for 25 years. I've got warehouse guys working 25–27 years. I'm not talking two or three. I'm talking 40 or 50.

Q: I love the story you told me about the guy who won the Lotto. You even took care of him, right?

A: Yeah, my boy, Ready G. He was playing the lottery for 25 years. He won six and a half million dollars in the lottery and I put him with my attorneys and my accountant so he wouldn't get skimped.

Q: So he's still driving the truck today, right?

A: No, he stayed with me for about eight months. But he got too much bull crap from his fellow workers, so he decided it was time to quit, to retire.

Principles and Philosophy

Q: So, Patrick, as a Republican, how do you feel about things like Affirmative Action? The Republican Party seems to be divided on that.

A: I'm a very strong supporter of Affirmative Action. I'm a child of immigrants. My father used to say to his sons, "Irish need not apply." I think that people, given the opportunity to become something, are smart enough to grasp it and do it. But if people are held back, and not given the opportunities, it's not right. So, I think that, I'm what you call a compassionate conservative. I believe in conservatism in certain aspects of politics, but also you have to be compassionate to our fellow Americans. People, veterans that come home should be well taken care of, for health reasons, for personal reasons, for educational reasons. I believe that it's the responsibility of our government to build a better society and how better are you going to improve it than to give people the opportunity to better themselves in life?

Q: So, do you think minorities going into business face more problems, more difficulties?

A: Actually, to tell you the truth, I don't. You say, what's a minority? African Americans, Chinese Americans, Korean Americans? You know, today you live and spend a lot of time in the city, you go into half the grocery stores in the city…the greengrocers are Koreans that are going in at 6 o'clock in the morning and working until 10, 11 o'clock at night. Well, when I was a kid, that's what the Italians did. And then they educated their children. And their children became the doctors and the lawyers and the businesspeople. And the same with the Koreans. I mean they are in there doing it. The African Americans today are, you see more and more prominent people.

And I've got to tell you the truth: I'm not sitting here and saying this to you because you're an African American or you're black—it makes me feel good when I see successful African Americans today. The night before last I was watching a ball game and I saw Derek Jeter walking out of the locker room—he looked like a million dollars. It makes me feel good. Listen, this country, anybody can be what they want to become if they have the ambition to go out and do it. I don't do business with people because they're green, white, yellow, or blue. I do business with people because they provide a service for me or they live up to what they say they're going to do. It's as simple as that.

Q: Well, I think African Americans and working people like yourself face the same problems in business that led me to ask you a lot of these questions. They don't have a lot of family support, they don't have a lot of start-up money, so they have to start on a shoestring budget and really work to build themselves up, so I think that's common throughout, people who don't have money or who don't—

A: One thing you have to learn early on is, don't feel sorry for the cards you got dealt. Go do something about it. Don't take—in my family, my entire family, which is quite extensive, I have 50 first cousins, 27 nieces and nephews. I come from a very big family. There were no businesspeople. I'm probably the only one. Irish Americans are not known for being entrepreneurs. In my industry, I'm probably one of the only Irish guys. The people in the trucking business and the warehouse business are predominantly Italian or Jewish. So I never looked at it that way—I always looked at it as a plus.

Today people have to realize that we're here together; we have to help each other wherever we can. You know, I mean, if you can give somebody an opportunity to make something of themselves, then you should do it. Let them try it. I think one of the biggest problems that minorities have, and again, I'll say it for myself as being one of them, my minority situation was I was cut from a different piece of cloth. When I wanted to go into business, my family said to me, "You're nuts, you're out of your mind, what are you doing that for?" I said, "Because I want to do it."

I remember my father asking me to become a New York City policeman. He said it's a great job, and all my friends that I grew up with became cops and firemen. I used to tell my father, "Dad, I got to find out what those guys who drive Cadillacs do, that's what I want to do." I found out that those guys were businesspeople, because it's very difficult in a lot of cases, you can make a good living working for somebody, but you're never going to really accumulate any wealth. And if you want to do that you have to do your own thing.

A lot of people say to themselves, "Well, I can't do that," and I say, "Well, why not? Why can't you do it? What's stopping you from doing it? You don't have any money? So what, try to figure out a way to get the money. Beg, borrow, or do whatever you've got to do to get it. Don't steal it. It's not a nice thing to do."

And you know, you can't sit there and feel sorry for yourself. You can't say, "Oh, shit, I'm black, I can't be in the trucking business" or "I'm black so I can't be a dentist." Bull crap. You can be anything you want to be—if you're honest, hardworking, and sincere. Sincerity shows out to people. You go into business with people and they know you're sincere and that you're going to do a job for them, they'll entrust their merchandise or their services, whatever it is, to you, as long as you live up to what you say you're going to do.

Q: Suppose you go to somebody and they entrust you. And you make a major mistake, an honest mistake that causes them to lose money. How do you rectify that?

A: If we make a mistake and cost our customer money, I have no problem. You have to do it a couple of times a year. We set up a big shipment for one of my big customers that left Hong Kong, the plane went into Japan, and the cargo got delayed there for four days and the customer lost the sale. I said to them, "Sell the merchandise at a markdown. Get what you can. Bill me the difference and I'll work it out for you." And that's exactly what I did. He was quite surprised I was willing to do that, and I said to him, "The way I look at my customers is that they are my partner. Without them, I cannot make money. Without them, I cannot operate a business or make a living. So I need to have them. I have to make sure that I can do everything that I can possibly do to make them successful, so I can continue doing this. And whatever that takes, we are willing to do."

Advice For New Entrepreneurs

Q: So, if you know a young 18- year-old or a 24-year-old Patrick, and they have this urge to get out and achieve, become an entrepreneur, what advice would you give them? You have given a lot already, but what advice would you tell a young person?

A: The strongest advice I would give to any young person that wanted to go into business is that you have to be prepared to give your soul. You have to take and put everything in life secondary and your business first. If you take care of your business and do it properly, the business will take care of everything else.

Q: So the advice you would give to a young person is that if you take care of the business, the business will take care of everything?

A: That's it. Don't be worried about parties. Don't be worried about holidays. Don't be worried about Sundays or Saturdays. Worry about one thing. Worry about your business. Make sure that you take care of that. And if you do that properly, you will be able to earn enough money to satisfy a lifestyle that will make you happy, something that you did.

A good example: a guy starts going into the painting business. Well, painters show up at nine o'clock in the morning, they go home at four. Start at eight, what's the difference? Get the job done quicker, you can do two jobs or three jobs. Just trying to give an example. It absolutely requires total, total dedication. And if you are prepared to do that and you do it, ninety percent of the chance you will be successful. The other thing that I strongly tell a lot of young people starting out is this: be prepared to give up five hard years of your life. Get established. It's written someplace, I don't know where it is, but it's written down someplace that it takes five years. You put in that first five years, don't look up, keep your nose to the grindstone. If you've got a half a brain, you should succeed.

Q: The average businessperson, they say, fails a couple of times before they get it right. So they could give five years, and then go under. A lot of time you start a couple of times, you fail. It might take three times for you to get it right.

A: There's an old saying, if you don't succeed at first, try and try again. I had a customer years ago who was actually a billionaire, Milton Petrie. He started a business called Petrie Stores. It was his fourth or fifth start-up. And he was 62 when he started it. He built it into a multibillion-dollar company. Just came up with a new concept and was able to do it. I mean there is no age to say when you are going to start.

You also need the support of your family. You need for the people you are going home to at night to understand exactly what you are doing, the sacrifices you are making. But if these people share in those sacrifices, they are willing to do it. I often felt bad with my sons, I wasn't there a lot. I missed a lot of ball games. I missed a lot of times that I could have spent with them but didn't. A couple of times a year, take them on extensive vacations so I could spend some quality time with them. Later on in life when they got bigger, I said, one day I sat them down, I always felt bad. I wasn't there a lot. And they laughed at me. They said, "Dad, are you kidding us? You did everything you possibly could do." So I am very fortunate there is nobody throwing it in my face.

Q: But you are very fortunate too because you didn't start with two or three—you pretty much started with the trucking business. It was kind of a straight line of development from there. You didn't flounder around a few times.

A: Business is opportunity. You go to a customer and they have a problem. And that problem absolutely presents you with an opportunity to fix it. If you can fix it then you've got the beginnings of a viable business.

SUMMARY

Patrick Heaney's stellar record as an entrepreneur proves that phenomenal business success can be achieved by anyone who has the desire, motivation, and drive to be their own boss. Despite having no formal education whatsoever, Patrick built a trucking company worth almost 100 million dollars. Now, at the age of 65, he's nurturing another successful business—an airfreight company poised to capitalize on the explosive growth of a global market.

Opportunities exist worldwide for entrepreneurs who learn to recognize—and can adapt their business models to accommodate—a changing marketplace. Between joint ventures, government programs, and foreign initiatives to open previously restricted markets such as China and Viet Nam, there has never been a better time to begin an entrepreneurial career, either locally or internationally.

CASE STUDY 5:
ELIZABETH
GONSALVES

INTRODUCTION

Elizabeth Gonsalves is a Registered Nurse and a native of Guyana. She graduated from Teacher's College and moved to the U.S. in 1976. After graduating from Helen Fuld School of Nursing (New York City), Elizabeth started Jos-el Care Agency in 1996. The Jos-el Care Agency provides nurses and medical care attendees to major hospitals and private patients. Elizabeth was a start-up entrepreneur without any business training. Through trial and error, plus hard work, she has built a multimillion-dollar annual revenue stream.

In the past couple of years, Elizabeth has broken new ground. In 2003, she diversified her business pursuits. As a certified minority vendor, her new company, Mediquip, sells medical supplies to governmental hospitals. Her staff is presently seeking export opportunities, particularly in the Caribbean region.

Although a busy businesswoman, Elizabeth donates a lot of her time and resources to charities. She purchases medical equipment with her own money and exports them to hospitals and nonprofits throughout the Caribbean region. Elizabeth is in demand as an inspirational speaker to business groups and struggling entrepreneurs.

THE INTERVIEW

Background/History

Q: I just want to ask you a series of questions about your entrepreneurial experiences. My first question is that, as a young girl, growing up in Guyana—I know you told me your father was in business—were you encouraged to pursue business? Did you work in his business? Were you kind of conditioned to the whole entrepreneurial legacy of your father? How did this whole thing start for you?

A: My father did have a business and I did work for him, but I can't actually say that he encouraged me to go into business also. What he did encourage us to do is to maintain certain principles. He never let us take anything for granted—that you are a child of the business, or you have a right to do anything you want, go to work at any hours, or spend how much you want. There was always strict discipline to that.

He always insisted that whatever you do, you need to do it the right away, and that when you work in a business, you don't think of yourself as a boss or an heir, but you just think of yourself as a person in that business that has to perform certain tasks to make the business work. And those were some of the principles we pretty much kept in mind. He never exactly said to us, "Well, you guys should go into your own business."

When you first start out—early in life when you grow up in your own business—you know you'll be better off with a job. There will be no responsibilities. But you don't stay on a job for very long when you tell yourself, I can do much better than just working at the job. Because when you apply the same principles to the job, you realize that sooner or later you become the key person there because you are doing the right thing.

Before you know it, you are taking a lot of responsibilities in that job and I think that's the point when you say, you know, I am doing all this and I'm still getting just the salary. I can possibly do it for myself. So you start having your first talks and doing your necessary research and making your plans for doing your own business. So home life has influenced it to some extent.

Q: The research shows that a lot of entrepreneurs tend to be children of entrepreneurs so that's why I wondered: did your background eventually influence you to pursue the entrepreneurial path?

A: I will say yes, because my father definitely was an entrepreneur. He had a general store. He had a farm. He had specialty crops. He had coffee and oranges and other things and he didn't just grow a farm. He decided he wanted to start processing, so he set up equipment to process coffee. It is interesting to see what a coffee berry looks like—how different it is to the powder you get in a cup or a tin or a package. So he set up that processing for his coffee.

We lived in a farming community and people also planted a lot of root vegetables that they ate. One of the popular root vegetables was yucca and people processed it to create flour to use as a staple instead of wheat flour. He also set up a processing center to do that.

He was always that sort of spirit where he got into a number of things that just went a little bit above what everybody else was doing. So I think that has influenced us to some extent, watching him become involved the way he was.

Q: Your sister is an entrepreneur. You are an entrepreneur, so would you make the point that it influenced the whole generation of siblings?

A: I think it did, because even my elder sister who doesn't live in this country is an entrepreneur. She owns a shoe business. She owns a shoe store. And my elder brother, who unfortunately is now ill, also was into business. The only one who is employed by somebody else is my youngest brother. Most of us did get involved in businesses.

Financing the Start-Up

Q: The hardest part in being an entrepreneur for a lot of people is to have the start-up money. From your dad's hard work, when you opened your own business, was that a financial legacy that you could draw on, meaning for your start-up money? Did your family help you financially in terms of getting your business up and going?

A: Actually, no. My start-up was a tough one, because it was pretty much my own effort and I have to plan my working life in a way that I can work *x* amount of hours. I did a lot of planning. I even made some investments before I actually went into business by getting a two-family house where I could rent a part and live in the other part so I am not plagued with the whole mortgage, which is a major expense for someone who isn't employed.

I started saving as much as I could and I tried to develop good credit. I made sure I was able to get a good credit line and that's how my actual start-up money came. It was just from salary, working one shift and working at the business another shift. And using my personal credit line, because in the earliest days of start-up, no one really wants to loan you any money. They look for experience oh so often. I got off the ground doing that and I did get help from relatives after, because what happens sometimes is that, even though you've made the start, you're off the ground, your expansion comes a little faster than you think it would, and you need that initial output of money before your profits come back. And I did get some help at that point from my relatives.

> Initially, self-financing is crucial. Loans guaranteed by the Small Business Administration are very expensive and time consuming.

Q: So for this type of agency, were your start-up costs very significant?

A: I would say the start-up cost was moderate because for one thing, you start in a small place so you have a small rent. And you start actually with your-self—as long as you have gotten all the required knowledge, you wear those several hats! Until you grow it alone to the point that you realize: OK, now I've had enough here, I can't do any more. You hire your first office person.

Well, of course you hire all the nurses in the earliest, take care of the number of referrals you get without any administrative staff—an office person—it's pretty much you alone until you say, OK, this is enough. And then you hire your first person to help you in the operation. After hiring that first person I think that was the plus because then I was able to not stay in the office and go out and do things that were more productive outside the office, and contributed to the growth of the business. So doing it that way I was able to keep the costs pretty low until we got to the point of raising enough to do it on a bigger scale.

Q: So for your start-up financing, you relied on yourself and at some point individuals helped finance you?

A: Yes, I relied on myself. It was not until we got so many referrals and we sent so many people out that our payroll began to become a lot larger than our receipts. And one of the interesting things about this business is that your receipts don't come until 30 days, 60 days, 90 days, and you have to be sure every week you have got that full payroll, so at that point I got some help, to be able to maintain the payroll.

Q: Any bank financing, anything like that?

A: At that stage, it was not the bank financing. I did take my personal credit line. I borrowed from it at that stage. In the earliest, it was not really the bank that financed it. Money saved and work doing things yourself, and trying to keep costs low.

Managing the Business

Q: They say the average entrepreneur fails three times before becoming success-ful. So what did you do before your present venture? Did you start a business prior to starting your present agency?

A: Actually, no. I came from my job into this business. I think another plus for me was that I worked in a similar situation and I was able to gain some hands-on experience.

My first thought about working for myself was not a nursing agency; I thought I'd probably do real estate. I did go ahead and get my license—salesper-son, broker—but I decided I didn't think I wanted to do that. I just thought that it took too much of running after people and going here and there and not get-ting enough results. Maybe if I had allowed it enough time to progress, but I thought I wanted to do something different, so the next thing I did was the nurs-ing agency.

Q: So Jos-el Care was the first entrepreneur business?

A: My first real business.

Q: What influenced you to start a nursing referral agency? I know that you're a nurse, but what were the main factors that led you to start Jos-el Care?

A: It was like I said: I was working in an agency. I did get to a supervisory position. I was carrying a lot of responsibilities and working real hard. I just sat one day and said, if I can do this for somebody else, I can do it for me. Because, for one thing, there were things I wanted to do differently that they didn't always agree with me about. Regardless of how hard I worked, I got still a salary and I said, I know I can do better than this. That's what led me to make a break-through and start. And I did leave and start doing that.

Q: You know, in business, they say you need a business plan—that if you plan to fail, then you failed to plan. So when you were developing Jos-el Care, did you develop an elaborate business plan with projections and all that?

A: I had a mental business plan. I never put it on paper. But in my mind I knew what I needed—I knew what I needed to get there. I knew where the possi-bility was that I could reach eventually, but it was all mental. I never sat down and wrote the business plan.

Q: That's a big debate in my field—about the importance of a business plan. I tend to agree with you. You can have a mental business plan, you can have an outline of points you want to do, but a lot of great entrepreneurs have never written great business plans.

A: I do want to agree with that. And, you know, when you are conscientious about what you are doing as you keep going, at some point if you think it's getting a little fuzzy in your head, you just sit back and you say, but you know this is where we want to be and this is where we are! And you think of what might be overwhelming you then or what you can cut back on. And you just put those ideas into action and say, this is what looks like it will work to move us from this point, or to simply buy things, and you do just that. But for me it has never been a fixed business plan that I followed and told myself, well, I am at every stage the way I wanted to be. It continued to be a mental thing.

Q: Have you ever formed something like an advisory board?

A: We do have what we call a Quality Assurance Board. I wouldn't particularly call it an advisory board. We do get some suggestions from time to time. But the Quality Assurance is more so a committee that examines the operations of the agency and makes…I wouldn't even say makes recommendations because there are fixed laws that we need to meet—fixed regulations, and most of these are defined by the Department of Health, which determines the way this should be done and the way we should do it. So basically what that Board does is examine how well we are conforming to that rule, and if we are not, ensure that corrections are made, that we stay on target.

Q: How did you, as a nurse, even though you had this entrepreneurial background, learn to become a sufficient manager of your business? I've read things where people, when they first started, didn't understand financial statements. How did you learn the language and skills that are necessary for you?

A: I must say there were a couple of supportive people along the way. I think I got a pretty good accountant in the earliest, and I'm one of those people who don't just sit with superficial knowledge. I didn't just let him hand me paperwork. I made sure everything I got was explained. I made sure that whatever he was doing he told me about it. And I'm pretty good at understanding and assimilating things if you tell me how. You know, I may not be able to do it, but I will have a general working knowledge. I will credit him with being one of the persons who has been pretty informative and supportive in the beginning stages, even at dealing with the IRS and all the other things.

Q: And you are pursuing your MBA?

A: Yes, I am.

Q: How is that empowering you? I mean, why are you doing that since you are already pretty successful?

A: It gives you a deeper understanding of, if I could say, the higher sophistication of business. It's not necessary for running this business, but it gives you a greater understanding of money and how money works. People may make money but you don't necessarily understand everything about money and how it works. And I thought at this point that would be helpful knowledge, because you do make some kind of profit and you want to make the right investments, and you want to have a good working understanding of what you're getting into.

I think that's just the curious part of me where I always like to have that working understanding. I feel it helps me to stay in control. You know, I find when I do that nobody can bring a story to you and, as they say in common terms, they can't easily pull the wool over your eyes, because you may not be able to find the fault, but you will have a general understanding that something isn't right, and you get somebody else, if it's necessary, to really check out what's going on and what needs to be corrected.

> Learning the dynamics of money will help you
> achieve broader financial goals.

Q: I've read of entrepreneurs, poorly educated people, poring over financial statements, balances—they just keep plugging away until they get it, until they understand it. So, I guess that's kind of the entrepreneurial development.

A: It is. It is. One thing I think I like about myself is that I get a quick grip of things. I will figure something out when I read it once or scanning it through. I don't necessarily have to stay with it a long time. I think that's one good thing that helps me.

Q: And before going back to work on your MBA, did you attend a lot of workshops, training workshops?

A: Not so much in accounting or even business management. For running the actual nursing agency, a lot of my experience came from the fact that I worked in an agency. There were finer points at the top that I probably didn't know, but the general working of and running of the agency came from that experience. And there were times when you felt you didn't have enough knowledge or enough specific knowledge...I did hire a consultant along the way and that helps you to correct and iron out some of the problems.

Q: Jos-el Care is now six years old? Seven years old?

A: It's about seven years old.

Q: In reflecting on the past, what were the major milestones or benchmarks? What were significant turning points for your agency?

A: We have had a gradual growth and I can't say that there is anything that happened very out-of-the-ordinary. We were fortunate to have a continuing progression. Like doubling our income year after year for several years. And I think when we got to about three years ago, we somewhat plateaued, and it didn't double at that point. We probably went up just a little more than that, or went down a little bit more. But our growth was really gradual. If you want to call it gradual on an annual basis we did see great spurts, so I'm not sure gradual is the proper word to use because we did double our income for a couple of years until, like I said, we got to a certain level where it then just went up a little bit, came down a little bit. It was almost what you would call an average for about three years.

Overcoming Obstacles

Q: In retrospect, what were some of the major mistakes or errors that you see in the past, things that you would do differently?

A: One of the things, if I were to do differently, and something that I will do to really move it from the plateau is to hire a good salesperson. Even though you did sales in the early stages, you can only stretch yourself out so much and you realize that you have to protect what you have. You have to make sure that it is functioning well, and you have to put your focus there. So you can't get out too much trying to get more when what you have is not doing well. So it takes away then from the marketing that you might have done in the beginning and it becomes necessary for you to get someone to market. And that's something I should have done even two years ago. I still don't know why I haven't done it. And in the earlier part one of the key persons you need to really look at is the person who does your billing. You want to stay on top of them because, you know, very small amounts lost can become significant over a period of time, and it's not that we've had a bad biller, but I think we did lose some money, which, if we had paid a little closer attention to it, would have been a lot better.

Q: Right. So you're not saying any major mistakes, any major setbacks, just basically growing pains.

A: No, we haven't had a major setback, growing pains has always been it. I think that maybe one of the reasons the business is plateauing right now is simply the unavailability of nurses. If we had had more nurses we could have done better. At this point I'm thinking, you can step up on your recruitment of nurses, but there's only so much anyway, you will get only your fair market share of nurses. So that's where that leaves us.

Q: I know you have 100 plus employees. What are the big headaches—the problems with dealing with 100 plus employees?

A: I have learned one thing as I talk with people all the time, is that if you are in a business where you deal with people, you have to be prepared for the challenges people present to you. It means you have to deal with all kinds of personalities, all kinds of demands, because some people are extremely demanding. You have to learn a lot of tact in dealing with people so that you can help them to see the point and not offend them. Your people skills greatly improve when you have that many employees and it's the only thing that helps you to keep everybody functioning and keep everybody at least reasonably satisfied. That you don't have explosive situations on your hands. People skills seem to be a key thing.

Q: Do you feel that minorities and women face more difficult challenges or problems in terms of starting up a business? If so, how?

A: I would say, yes, because for one thing, I find minorities don't always get the amount of support they would like to have. Not from their relatives, not from whatever resource they have to go to. People always question you a little more. You have got to really prove that you are worthy of whatever. You have to make sure you know it very thoroughly, which I think is a good thing, because I don't want to do it any other way than the way of authority. But you see other people getting the same things that you've been asking for much more easily and without that much questioning.

I like to make my negatives positives, and what I usually say is: this may be good, because I wouldn't take anything for granted. I will do what I need to do the right way and it will save me from a lot of pitfalls later on. But there is definitely a visible difference between the way people make demands on other people as they do minorities.

Q: Like other minority entrepreneurs, do you face a lot of family distractions and obligations?

A: I must say I have been a little fortunate in that respect because my immediate family has been reasonably supportive, and I don't have too many relatives beyond my immediate relatives. Our families are not very large. I guess that is part of the way I think. I find myself voluntarily doing a lot of giving, simply because you see so much need, you feel that if you have even a little to afford, and that little sometimes goes a long way for people, you feel like you want to do it. But my relatives, and again I said there were not many, I can almost say one sister, was willing to do what she can in whatever way, if ever I had a need that she could possibly fulfill.

Q: Well you kind of touched on my next point. I know that you are very active in different civic/community/humanitarian organizations.

A: Yes, I am.

Q: Yes, very much so. Has this helped you in business, your activity in these social community organizations? Has it helped you in terms of business, your bottom line?

A: Now, that's an interesting question. Financially, in some ways, you might say it's not helping the bottom line because you are giving out. But at the same time, you happen to meet people when you do this, and some people happen to recognize what you do and you form relationships, and from the relationships it sometimes opens up other business opportunities, and that pretty much is a good thing. When you start, at least me when I started out, that was not my intention at all. I did what I thought I saw needed to be done, but it did come over with that positive side effect.

Q: The reason I asked you is because I think a common characteristic of bootstrap entrepreneurs is that they tend to be more active in their social environment than these other big Harvard-type people. And by being active, they develop a lot of relationships that are beneficial for them. And in the long run, it does seem to help their bottom line. I am just speculating—asking you.

A: That is a good observation because, like I said, the fact is that some people do recognize what you do and it does open up opportunity. Just getting to know people, because a fact we have to face is that so many things in this world are network oriented. And meeting people can do something positive for your network and become part of your network.

Q: I am aware that you are very active in all kinds of organizations. How do you see synergy or linkage between all your international interests and organizations and your domestic ones? Is that something that is separate, or do you see that as dovetailing at some point?

A: It depends on the way you look at it. It may not necessarily bring financial gain at all times. It does sometimes, but in some ways it does one good thing, because you are seen as a goodwill ambassador, which gives a good impression of you, your country, and everything else. Strange enough, sometimes it ends up in some sort of financial gain, but even when it doesn't, it creates that sense of communication and goodwill, which can be very positive.

Looking Toward The Future

Q: You are still a young lady; what are your future plans or goals?

A: I do plan to stay active in business for a couple more years, at least, because when you are in business at my level and you are initiating things, you have no choice but to be active, because you go through again setting the groundwork, building the framework, and it involves a lot of you. One of the good things—it becomes a little easier because you bring with it practical experience you have gained over your early years as an entrepreneur. And it brings a youth that is a little more prepared to take on a project simply because of the knowledge and the degree of comfort you bring with it. I am planning to do a couple more things.

Q: Will it be more business or more social?

A: I think as I get older and I set a couple of goals, it's going to be a little more social. I can see myself volunteering some more and spending time in situations where people need help rather than being in active business.

Advice For New Entrepreneurs

Q: So, I know your niece. If your niece came to you and said, "Auntie, I want to go into business. I decided my path is an entrepreneurial one." What advice would you give her or to young people today?

A: I'd say, "Yes, if you think you want to do it, you sure can." I'll just give them just a little bit of knowledge they need to have, that anytime you are going to go into business, it's not just a fantasy, but I will try to make them aware of the real things you have to face, and I'll try really to advise them on what they need to do. You shouldn't want to go into business unless you have a very good knowledge of how the business operates, because I always feel—I know there are many wealthy people out there who have money and decide, I want to invest, and they hire people who they think have knowledge to do it. If you are not a person who is in that category, I will say, make sure you learn well about the business before you go into it, probably work in that business that somebody owns and learn what you need to learn before you go in.

And be prepared to become committed. Be prepared for the hard work. Be prepared for the ups and downs because it's not always smooth and sometimes you are going to think you're going under, but if you just hang in there, continue to do the right thing, you will be successful in the end.

Q: Any other points you would tell a young person?

A: Nope. I would encourage them generally, and I think those are some of the key things if you are going to actually start your own business.

Q: The point you made, too, is that, you pretty much self-financed your business, so I think you would tell them, too: make some money, get your credit in order.

A: Definitely. And I think when you self-finance, it's less pressure on yourself. You don't want to start out being plagued with the fact that I have to meet loan installments, I have to do this, I have to do that. It's an extra pressure and stress that you can do well without. It certainly makes the growth a little slower but even now as I'm a little more experienced, in looking back, I appreciate the slow road. You learn so many things along the way. So by the time you had spent your first three years and then you probably didn't go as far as you thought you would, you did have so much experience that from the third year on, you could have made so much a difference, in larger investments if you were going to make mistakes, at least they wouldn't hurt you that much. When you make the mistakes in the earlier stages and it's small, you can keep moving, but you don't want to have those major mistakes in the later stages. So I didn't even feel disadvantaged for having tried to set my own financial goals and raising my own finances to get off the ground.

Q: You never had a partner in your business. Why not? I know people have different views on that.

A: Maybe if I go into a really big business later, I may consider a partner. But it'll have to be a real consideration of knowing the person or the persons, a clear understanding of what they are going to bring to the business and all that sort of thing. It's not something that it's out of my thoughts. Surely enough, if I do have a business that's big enough, or should I say, if we did want to go into something that is really large, I'm quite open to working with a partner.

Q: I want to say I appreciate your time; thank you for the interview.

SUMMARY

Elizabeth Gonsalves joined the ranks of the self-employed for the same reason that many entrepreneurs do: she was working for someone else when she realized she could do the same thing, but for her own company. She wisely began by saving her money and building her credit while still employed so that when she finally took the plunge, she was able to self-finance her business. This allowed her to grow her business gradually as she learned the financial and business administration skills necessary to take her company to the next level.

By starting small and growing gradually, Elizabeth was able to maintain her company's financial stability. This is an important strategy in an era when many entrepreneurs allow their company to balloon out of control—growing beyond their administrative capacity until finally the business implodes. Hers is a study in discipline and managed growth. Of all the participants interviewed, Elizabeth is the only one who is pursuing a higher academic degree to give her an even greater edge in the marketplace.

CASE STUDY 6: JOE CORCHADO

INTRODUCTION

Joe Corchado is the founder of JFD Sales Consulting Services Corporation. He has more than thirty years of experience in the office furniture field and has worked for several of the larger office furniture dealerships in the New York City area. Having gone as far as he could within the standard office furniture dealership, Joe decided to start his own firm. He began in 1997 and now has offices in New York and New Jersey, as well as four warehouse facilities. His company generates millions of dollars in annual revenue. He is very active in several Hispanic and minority business associations and is in demand as a speaker on minority business issues.

THE INTERVIEW

Background/History

Q: Joe, there is an argument that entrepreneurs are made, not born. So my first question to you is: Does your family have an entrepreneurial background? Did you come from a family of businesspeople?

A: No, I think I'm the first generation that has broken into the business world. My mother came from Puerto Rico in the late '60s, and when she came here she was a factory worker. She used to sew gloves in a factory and back then, the wages were very, very poor. And in looking at my mother's struggle, like most immigrants that come to this country, I decided that I was going to do something different than she did. So the belief that entrepreneurs are born and not made—I don't think so. I think it might be a combination of both, but the need sometimes outweighs the idea that you've got to be born into business.

Q: When you started business, did you receive any assistance from your family—financial assistance, any kind of assistance?

A: No, not really. I had some money saved up from working throughout the years, and when I started my business in 1997, I started it with, I think, 25 or 30 thousand dollars. And in this business that we're in, the majority of the companies that get into this line of work, in order for you to own a company or dealership, you need at least a half a million dollars to start. But we were fortunate that we had contacts with clients, contacts with manufacturers, and my investment of 30 thousand dollars was enough for me to get the organization started.

We started with two people in '97 with a small office that was maybe 500 square feet, maybe less than that, and now, in 2006, which is nine years later, we have 12 employees and we average anywhere from eight to ten million dollars a year. So it's been a lot of work and a lot of—I believe I have been successful. It hasn't been easy because we have not had any support from major companies. All the success we've had has been self-made, self-motivated.

Q: As a successful businessperson, what obligations do you have to your family? You are a businessman but you are also a family person. What obligations do you have to your extended family?

A: When I started the business, I sat down with my family and we talked about the business, and we came to the decision that if I wanted my business to have a piece of the American dream, if I wanted to have my family move into a better home, drive a better car, shop in the malls, like most Americans do, there were sacrifices that had to be made. So the agreement was that my wife was going to be taking care of the kids at home and taking care of the family, and I was going to focus my attention on business.

When you are an entrepreneur, there are certain sacrifices that you have to do. And in my case, the sacrifice has been in not being with my family all the time and being the 9-to-5 father that most people are. With me, I don't have a schedule. My workdays are from six in the morning until seven, eight o'clock at night. So my contact with my immediate family has not been as much as I want it to, but you have to make certain sacrifices if you want to acquire some kind of success in the Big Apple.

Q: For many non-minority entrepreneurs, their families stepped up to the plate, gave them start-up funds. If the business was running dry, they injected cash. It seems that successful minority businesspeople, like yourself, are burdened with a lot of family obligations and pressure.

A: That's correct—you are absolutely right. Since I am the first generation businessperson, I didn't have anybody that could come to my rescue whenever I had any kind of problems, whether they were emotional or financial. I had to pretty much do it on my own and rely on people that were close to me, people that knew me, to keep giving me the encouragement that I needed to continue working hard, fighting for every piece of business that we get. Nobody has given us anything for free. All the business we get, we compete for. We have established relationships that have taken years to build, and all this has come from a lot of hard work and a lot of energy spent in building up the business.

I think, as people who are immigrants to this country, it is very hard for us to have what other people may have that go to Harvard or Yale or Princeton, and that's wealthy families that can pump into the business, either cash or management or experts or whatever might be needed for them to be successful. When it comes to us, I think we pretty much have to do it all on our own.

Q: On the other side, I know other entrepreneurs, even as they are striving to help family members that may go into prison or deal with drugs, they not only have the business pressure, they also have these personal/family pressures too. And that seems to be a big difference between the street entrepreneurs and the other types.

A: Well, you know, being that we are from neighborhoods that are not the wealthiest in the world, we do have to deal with poverty. We have to deal with drugs. We have to deal with prostitution. We have to deal with teenage pregnancy. We have to deal with all the common woes that society has today, especially when we come from neighborhoods that are not very affluent. So besides the business stress and pressures, we also have our family's stress and pressures that we have to deal with on a daily basis. Sometimes you can have the best family in the world, but you still live in an environment that may not be the best in the world, and it's around you. That environment is around you, and you have to deal with all the issues that are part of society today. You are absolutely right.

Q: Are you a serial entrepreneur? Is this your first business? They say the average entrepreneur starts three times and fails before they are successful. Do you have any other skeletons in your closet where you started businesses before, or is this your first?

A: No, I do not. This is just the first business that I have ever gone into. I think the reason we have been successful is because before I went into business, I spent a lot of years in this business, so I had a lot of experience associated with the sales and processing of the items that we promote here in the company. Where we had a very difficult time was with the management side of the company, because all the years I spent was at the sales end, and going from a salesperson to a business owner is totally a different story. So in my case, not only did we have financial difficulties in the beginning, but we also had, and we continue to have, managerial problems, where we try to get the right managers to help me grow the business, and that is something I think every business, whether you are a large business or a small business, always has. Find the right qualified people to come on board and help build the company.

Q: Describe your business, JFD Sales. What exactly do you do?

A: JFD Sales is a company that specializes in the retail market of office furniture. And when we started the business, we decided to focus on the government, the healthcare and the educational business, and I did that because I felt that this particular business was not getting the attention necessary from companies like us. Most of our competitors, they focus on the corporate side of the business. They love to deal with the AT&Ts, the Prudentials, the Verizons, because of the status and the symbols that these companies represent. We opted not to do business with these people. We opted to do business with the government sector where it might not be prestigious, but they still spend a lot of money. We opted to do business with the healthcare industry. While it is not prestigious like doing business with an AT&T or Prudential or Verizon, it is still a very lucrative business.

It doesn't matter what market you're in, if there is a building being built, you need furniture. And that's the reason I think we decided to stay within this particular market. So we design, we deliver, we install the product. We network with other entrepreneurs a lot, especially if they are minority owned. And we deal with the labor issues at the site. We always pay the prevailing wage, which is a requirement from the people I do business with. So pretty much again, JFD is a turnkey office furniture company. What we provide our clients with is total customer satisfaction.

Go with what you know. Stick to very narrow products and markets; you will be more successful by developing experience and a reputation in a specialized niche.

Managing the Business

Q: How did you, as an entrepreneur, learn the language, the skills of business—how to read a balance sheet, how to deal with the IRS, how to read financial statements?

A: When I first decided to go into business, I was told something that I took to heart—that in order for me to be successful in my business venture, I needed two important ingredients: a very good attorney, and a very good accountant. And I went out and hired, which I thought to be and they still are, the best attorneys and the best accountants, and although I didn't have the legal expertise, they had it. And although I didn't have the expertise of accounting, they had it. So those two people that I've had for a long, long time, they are the ones that have helped me through the legal and the accounting process a business requires. Also, when I started the business, I brought on board a lady that was the controller of my former company, and she came on board with the vision of helping me grow this business. So, the most important thing is that if you don't know something, either you learn it, or you get surrounded with people that do know. And I think that is the secret to success.

Q: What about self-empowerment? I notice that a lot of entrepreneurs do a lot of reading. They go back and take workshops to improve their skill level. Is that something you have actively done in the past, or are still in the process of doing?

A: Well, to tell the truth, because my time is so important and I'm always concentrating on getting business opportunities or maintaining business opportunities, I really have not had the chance to spend a lot of time in these workshops that sometimes are crucial to a business. Again, in my case, I decided to go and either hire or contract the experts that I needed to grow my business while I focused my time on getting the business. You can't do everything. You can't do everything in the world. To me, I see myself as a conductor. I don't play the instruments, but I conduct the music. Like in an orchestra, you have a lot of people playing instruments and only one guy conducting the whole symphony— that's me. I'm the conductor. I'm the maestro. But I have a lot of people that work with me, or for me, who will help me achieve the goal of bringing that fine piece of music to the ears of my clients.

Q: A lot of entrepreneurs I've dealt with have not been very successful in dealing with the government process, with government agencies. Most people, when you talk to them they say, "I can't waste my time dealing with the Port Authority. It's too much red tape." Why have you been so successful…what are your keys to success in dealing with government agencies to earn revenue, to generate revenue?

A: What I've found is that, in order for you to be successful, you've got to understand the product you're selling—that's number one, and number two, you've got to understand who your consumers are. Number three, you've got to understand how do they purchase. Those are the three secrets for you to be successful: One, know your product; Two, know the people who are buying your product; and Three, you have to understand how they buy your product. Once you understand those three things, then it's a matter of putting a plan together and sticking to the plan and making it a success. And I think that's what has made us a success. I know the product that I sell. I might not be the most eloquent person in the world or the smartest person in the world, but I do know my product. I know what it is, and I know what its capability is. I know what it could do for my client. I know the advantages and disadvantages.

You have to know your product first. And once you know your product, then you have to find out who purchases your product. Who is the client? Who are they? What are they? And once you find out who they are, the next thing is, how do they buy it? And once you understand how they buy, then you are able to formulate a plan of how to sell it to them. And that's been my secret and my success.

Q: A lot of red tape.

A: Red tape. There's red tape in everything. There's red tape in going to the supermarket and collecting all the things you're going to buy—you've got to get on line, pay for it, and then you've got to pull your cart home. So there is red tape in everything. If people think that they should go into business and they are not going to find red tape, then they shouldn't be in business, because they have a misconception of what the real world of business is about. So there is red tape in everything. It's a matter of understanding how to get around the red tape. If there's a wall in front of you, there's three ways of getting through that wall. You either go through it, which you can't, so you go over it, or you go on the left of it, or you go on the right. Three ways. You go over it, left, or right. But you manage to get over the wall, and that's the same thing about business. Business is the wall. But then how do you get over the wall? That's what people really have to understand.

Q: When you first developed JFD Sales, did you spend a lot of time writing out and developing a very formalized business plan?

A: No, not really. What I did was I kept in mind those three things that I was mentioning to you. In business, in order for you to have a business, you have got to have sales. So I always focus on that side. And then I hire people that handle the other aspects of the business. So I didn't have...I didn't develop these great master plans.

It's funny. If you go to networking events or classes or whatever, they tell you that, in order for you to be successful, you have to have this big master plan. You've got to do this business plan—you've got to do this, you've got to do that. And that's great. But I think the most important thing is that you have to have the ambition to go out and get the business. Once you get the business you can always develop all the others.

> You should always be selling. Sell yourself and your product. Overcome your fear and reluctance because bringing in new business will always be your responsibility.

You can have the greatest business plan in the world, but if you're not a go-getter, what's the use of having that? In my case, I focused on getting the business, and then I worried about how I was going to spend the money, and where I was going to spend the money. But in order for you to figure out where you are going to spend it and how you are going to spend it, first you need the money. So that is what I focus on: getting the money, and then I figure out how to spend it. I think it's important for people to have knowledge of business plans. I think it's important for people to have knowledge of finance, how to read a balance sheet, how to read a financial statement. I think it's important for that. But those things can be gotten; they can be bought. You can bring others on board to do that. What you need is the ambition and the mentality of going out and getting the business you're focusing on. Once you get that business, you can hire the other people to do the work for you. But you still need to know what's going on so you can take a look and make sure you are supervising the people that are working for you. So you need both.

Q: So as a veteran now, so to speak, what do you spend most of your time doing?

A: Most of my time right now is spent still getting more business and administrating the office and taking care of the business and making sure everything goes right, making sure that our clients are happy and watching the bottom line. As I get older, the tasks just become greater because, in the beginning, I used to just focus on generating the sales volume. Now it's the sales volume, and paying the employees, and making sure we have enough to keep going.

Lessons Learned

Q: What do you think is the biggest mistake, or the biggest errors you have made since starting your own business, and how did you recover from those errors or mistakes?

A: Well, sometimes the biggest mistake is trusting people you shouldn't trust, or putting too much into the hands of people you think you can trust, and then finding out you shouldn't have trusted them. Sometimes it kind of leaves a bad taste in your mouth about trusting people in general, but I believe there is goodness in every person and although I have had bad experiences with some people, I've had good experiences with others. So the biggest mistake that I've made is relying on people I thought I could count on, then having it not really work out for me. Sometimes, because we're family-oriented people, we think that because we are running a business, we could bring in family. And that's the biggest mistake that we do. And then we might pay them top dollars because they are our family, but then when you need to correct or to change or need to do something, it's very difficult, because they are family. So these are some of the mistakes that I have gone through in my career.

Other mistakes have been not getting involved in the process, let's say the political process, because most business in New York is politically motivated, and unless you get involved or unless you belong somewhere and you belong to some organization, you find yourself fighting an uphill battle all by yourself. So in business you need friends, and sometimes friends come from the same people that are around you.

Q: I'll come back to the political process in a minute, but could you maybe elaborate a little more on the mistakes in trusting people, or is it too personal?

A: No. The mistakes in trusting people in my case were people who came to me and said, "Joe, I'm great at doing this; I know a lot of people. I could bring you business, and for that, I would like to come and work for you. I'd like to get paid $60,000 a year" or something like that. And you take a chance because you are friendly with the people or because you trust them, you bring them on board. They are in the organization four or five months, you lay out $30,000 in advance but then there's no business coming in. So those are the mistakes that I'm talking about—bringing people on board who claimed they could do things, but they really can't.

Q: So any depression from that?

A: Oh yeah, definitely, especially business. Money is very hard to come by and when you expend $50,000 or $100,000 in people that are supposed to be generating income for you and then you find out that they are not really as good as they claim they are, it's a loss that you take, and sometimes it's hard to recover from those losses, especially if you are a small business.

Q: I know that you are very active in a lot of organizations, like National Minorities Suppliers Government Council, Hispanic Chamber of Commerce. How have these organizations benefited your business pursuits?

A: To tell you the truth, they really have not helped me any. I think I do it more of a way of giving back to the community. It's almost like being a philanthropist; I guess that's what you call it. I help other business owners understand how to do business with the government. I help other business owners understand some of the pitfalls that they are going to encounter if they decide to go into business. The organizations that I am associated with haven't really given me any business, or helped me get any business, but what they have done is help me understand who I am, where I came from, and the fact that I could help other people achieve the same goals that I have achieved.

My mentality is that the more minorities there are in business, the better off we all are. So it's not enough to have just a couple, but as many as we can. And if I could help them understand how to get into business, how to maintain the business, and some of the pitfalls that they have to look out for, well, that's the reason why I do it. So I belong to all these organizations because I like to help people.

For many years now I have tried to put people together—and that's the most difficult thing in the world to do—put people together to try to look at the dream of being in mainstream America, to take advantage of the economics in America. But that's the most difficult thing in the world. That's one of the reasons why I belong to so many groups, because I try to network, I try to bring them together. I try to talk to them and see if there is a way that we could work together.

Q: So your community activism has not financially benefited you?

A: It has nothing to do with financial rewards.

Q: It hasn't increased your bottom line at all.

A: No, on the contrary. It has cost me money. Because all these organizations I belong to they have a membership, they have fundraisers, and I try to contribute as much as I can to them.

Q: So do you believe that minorities, women, face more difficult challenges or problems of going into business and, if so, why?

A: I think we need to reclassify the statement you just made. I think that minority women and I think that minority—

Q: I said minorities *and* women.

A: So if you say minorities and women, with that statement you have Anglo women, and I think that if you take a look at New York City, or maybe America in general, the people that do well are Anglo businesses, and then the second are Anglo females, and then the third and fourth are minorities and then female minorities. So that I believe that if you are a female minority or a minority person, you do have a lot of struggles and hurdles to overcome rather than the other people that are in business.

Q: What would you identify as maybe the top three hurdles that people would have to overcome?

A: Well, the first of the top three is knowledge. I feel that because we just got into the mentality of becoming business owners in the past maybe 20, 30, 40 years, most of us have always been workers, not businesspeople. So I feel that the rest of the world, the non-minority, has had an advantage over us for the longest time. Why I feel that Anglo women have an advantage over most of the minority female population or minorities in general is because the Anglo women are married to the Anglo men. And who has had the biggest opportunity in America? The Anglo men, and after the Anglo men, who comes next? The Anglo women. Again, I don't want to sound racist or anything, but it's purely economics. They have had a much better opportunity and a much longer time at being business owners than we have. And that's one of the biggest hurdles. So first is knowledge.

The second is finance, and the third is just the pressures, social pressures that we have as minorities that other people do not have. So I think those three are the biggest problems that we face as challenges.

Q: Getting back to the point we spoke about earlier. How can you navigate the political waters? New York is a very political town. Democrat, Republican. How do you make progress in the water filled with sharks?

A: I think that when it comes to politics you have got to be very, very careful, and like you said, when you are in waters infested with sharks, you just have to make sure you don't become the bait. So in my case, I think that I have been successful because I am nonpolitical. In other words, I have friends that are Republicans and I have friends who are Democrats. And I try to see them as people, not as politicians. And whenever they need help, I'm there, whether as a Republican or a Democrat. And the help could be in any kind of form. It could be because they may have a fundraiser, because they are doing something great for the community. When that happens, I don't see politics. I see someone trying to do something for the community. And that person may be a Democrat or they might be a Republican. So I try not to see it in the political venue. I try to see it as people trying to help other people out. And that's why I've tried to maintain myself kind of neutral when it comes to that.

Looking Toward The Future

Q: So you are still a young man. What are your future plans?

A: My future plan is to keep growing this company and, like I said, first generation businessperson, my son will be graduating from high school this year and attending Howard University in August and he is looking into the opportunity of getting into business, so hopefully by the time he graduates from college, he might be able to take this company to the next level. He'll be the second generation of business entrepreneur in my family, and hopefully he will do a lot better than I have. And he might—I'm sure he will—be more successful than I will be. And when his son comes, there will be third generation and a fourth. And by that time we will probably catch up with the rest of the world. We will be in a better position than we are right now.

Q: This is a side point. When I was a kid growing up in Texas, we had all black supermarkets because of segregation, black supermarkets, black stores, so we had our own economy. With the development of the big McDonalds, the civil rights movement, integration, we lost a whole legacy of black entrepreneurship, a whole generation. Would that be similar to the Hispanic experience, or is that more unique to blacks?

A: I think so, I think so. I think that when a lot of Hispanics came to this country, they kind of settled in the barrio, upper Manhattan. But as people get successful, they start moving away, and other cultures come in. And so I think that dividing people, or spreading people, or taking people from one area to another, or people growing intellectually or financially, they decide to move. It's good, but it also hurts the neighborhood because the money doesn't stay within the neighborhood. It goes away. So I think you're right.

I don't know if having everybody in one place is good or if it's bad, but I think you're right. It has hurt people as a people. I don't know what the answer is. In my mind, I have helped myself, and I always said that when I got to a level that I could help others, I would do that. So I've always helped people as I have grown, and now that I am at a level that I think I am somewhat successful, then I am always looking to help other people out. And I think when you have that mentality, then you don't have to worry about whether you are all in the same place or whether you are not in the same place, because as you grow, you help others grow. It will achieve the same thing as everybody being in one place and keeping the money within the community.

Advice For New Entrepreneurs

Q: What advice would you give a young person who wants to start up in business in 2006, 2010, whatever? What advice would you give them?

A: The same three things, the advice I mentioned that I had thought about when I started in business: Understand the product you want to sell, understand who the consumer is, and understand how they purchase the item. It doesn't matter what kind of business you are going into, whether it's a retail food chain or whether it is insurance or whether it's an automobile dealership, whatever it is, you need to know your product, know the people that are buying it, and know how to sell it. Those are the three keys. Once you know the three keys, you will be successful. That and determination.

You've got to be determined, and you've got to keep at it and keep at it until you become successful. It's almost like working a gold mine. There's no assurances or guarantees that you are going to hit it big, but if you keep working the gold mine, sooner or later, you are going to hit it big. And that's the same thing with business. You've got to keep at it and keep at it and sooner or later you will have success. That is the advice I give my son. And that's the advice I would give to other young people too.

Q: What other advice do you give to minority youth interested in business?

A: You know, I think people associate business with success, and that's the reason they get into business—they want to be successful. But I think success is measured in many different ways. You don't have to be in business by yourself to be successful. So what I would say to young people is that they should look at different options, not just focus on one item.

I did this because this is all I know. I didn't have a lot of options. I was forced to understand this business. And after I understood it and I worked, then I said, OK, I don't want to do this on my own. But it hasn't been easy. One of the keys to success is working together with other people. So perhaps what any young entrepreneur might do is, think about what level of success they're looking for. Is it success or having their own business? Because success doesn't always come by having your own business. Sometimes it's a headache and a pain. I was making more money when I was in sales than I am now. People think that because you have a business, you are a rich guy. No. You've got payroll, you've got health insurance, you've got rent to pay.

Q: You are paying everybody else before you pay yourself.

A: Exactly. Sometimes that's not success. That's headaches. But I've reached successes financially when I was in sales and I wanted to do something different. I wanted to own my own business. But that's a choice I made. And it's not an easy choice to make. So I would say to someone looking to get into business, take a look at other opportunities. What are you looking for—success? Being able to make money so you can live the way you want, or is it that you want to own your own business and all the headaches that go with it? What is it that you're looking for?

Q: I developed my questions to reflect the path of development of street smart entrepreneurs. So is there anything else you would like to add?

A: No, I think that there is merit in both sides. Just because a person is born into a family that is affluent, you can't blame them for that. More power to them. There's merit in that and there's merit in what we do. I think it's just a matter of understanding what you have to work with, then work with that, whether you are rich or you are poor. It's just a matter of working at it, and developing strategies, and bettering your life. Sometimes being affluent doesn't mean that you are happy. It's finding happiness in what you do, in whatever that might be. That's the only thing I could say.

Q: Well thank you very much for your time, Joe; I appreciate it.

SUMMARY

Joe Corchado achieved success by utilizing his existing knowledge base and leveraging it to carve his own niche in a much broader market. His business philosophy, to which he attributes his success, is simple: 1) know your product, 2) know your customer, and 3) understand how and why your customers buy. This simple formula can be applied to any type of business, and is, in fact, the foundation of a solid marketing plan.

Joe's advice to young people who might be considering an entrepreneurial path mirrors the sentiment shared by every other participant in these interviews: you've got to dedicate yourself to your business and be persistent in your efforts. No matter what method you use to measure success, you've got to be happy doing whatever it is that you do.

CASE STUDY 7: DAWN BENNETT

INTRODUCTION

Dawn Bennett is a registered nurse from Jamaica. She arrived in this country with just her suitcase. She currently owns three Golden Crust franchises and is a member of its Executive Board. In addition, Ms. Bennett operates an assisted living center in Baltimore, Maryland.

She employs local residents and is active in the Caribbean and African-American communities. Dawn gives back by one-on-one mentoring for minorities interested in business development, especially franchise ownership. She also serves as a motivational speaker for community and entrepreneur training workshops and seminars.

THE INTERVIEW

Background/History

Q: The first question I would like to ask you is: As a child in Jamaica, what really influenced you to become such an independent and resourceful person?

A: In Jamaica, we didn't have a lot of anything and we had no government to depend on, so you had to basically make it on your own, doing the best you can. I had a brother who lived in Maxfield Avenue, and as a teenager I remember him having a restaurant, a bar, and also a meat store. So that was my first example of business being in my family. That inspired me. I thought it was something good. I am the only girl from my mom. I have three brothers.

I migrated…I got married when I was 19 years old. I migrated to this country, went to college, and became an RN. While working two jobs and raising my children, while working as a nurse, because of my leadership skill that I acquired while being a charge nurse, I also wanted someday to open up a business of my own, not just for owning a business, but so that I could empower my community, maybe provide local jobs, maybe take an abandoned store in the community and renovate it, rebuild it, and start a business.

Q: Your extended family then—except for your brother who was an entrepreneur that inspired you—doesn't really have a history of entrepreneurship. I did notice when I was in Jamaica that most of the small shops seemed to be owned by non-blacks. I saw a lot of Chinese people, Syrians, and so forth owning the stores, but I didn't notice so many blacks owning businesses. Here in the U.S. it seems to be just the opposite. Jamaicans, to me, are the leading edge of this whole rise in black entrepreneurship. Why do you think this is the case?

A: You're right. I remember, growing up as a child in Jamaica, that there were little mom-and-pop shops that had a little hole in the wall and they would sell ethnic authentic food, but the major stores were owned by Indians or Syrians. So we knew what it was to have little shops, not any designer shop—maybe a family would live upstairs and downstairs they would open up a little area. A lot of time it was more soul food. Maybe Mommie is a good cook, and the neighborhood knows she is a good cook, so she would put out product; but you're right, on a big scale, if you go into the mall, if you go into the resorts, there you see a lot of foreigners opening businesses.

One other thing is that a lot of time it's about finances; a lot of folks not able to get the funds to open up businesses. In this country, however, most of us aspire to own our own home, like we did back in the Caribbean. The difference is here your home will build equity and out of the equity you could take money and start a business.

Q: But what is it in Jamaica—cultural legacy or whatever—that drives the trend I've noticed in working with so many entrepreneurs throughout the country, that a large percentage of the business leaders and entrepreneurs of tomorrow tend to be Jamaicans? What influences that?

A: I agree, and if they are not Jamaican, they are maybe children of Jamaicans. I notice the next generation of Jamaican, their children are aspiring to be entrepreneurs. Ambition is in us, the drive, the hardworking. I'm not sure exactly.

Q: My friend, Lorna, was here this weekend and I asked her the same question. Besides some of the things you mentioned, she thought that the influence of

Marcus Garvey has been deeply implanted in Jamaican people, even though Jamaicans may not talk about him a lot, some of his ideas have been passed on from generation to generation. So she also added that as a factor.

A: Absolutely. It's funny you should say that, because when I was visiting Jamaica, I went to the bookstore at the Norman Manley Airport and gathered a couple of books that were children-oriented, but one was a biography of Marcus Garvey. And I was excited to bring it back here and pass it on to my grandchildren and my goddaughter. Because in the book he spoke about entrepreneurship. He talked about how we must rise up as a great people. And you're right, I must pay homage to Gary Bird of WLIB [New York radio station].

When I came to this country, I was not so conscious and I did not know too much about Marcus Garvey, but listening to the Gary Bird experience as a visiting nurse driving through the streets of Brooklyn, I would sit in my car trying to make a visit, but I was compelled to sit and listen to him when he would bring excerpts or more information to me about Marcus Garvey.

Another person that also inspired me was the guy that wrote the book about the Kwanzaa, and the principles, Dr. Karenga. He spoke about getting your community to make it more beautiful. He spoke about opening businesses, doing business with your people, providing jobs for your people. He spoke about respecting the leaders, whether they were teachers or lawyers or doctors in our community. So that was also something that inspired me to go on and take a part, open up my first store in a part of Brooklyn that at the time was not so popular. But I put $150,000 that I got from equity out of my home, and put it in my community.

Q: So my next question is this: How are you passing this legacy on to your children and grandchildren?

A: I am not only passing the legacy to my children and my grandchildren, but also my nieces and nephews that are involved with me. They are part of the business. They are involved in the business. I am encouraging them also to not only be consumers, but also to produce at their own businesses, provide jobs for their community, and I am impressing on them that it's part of their heritage— they must do that. They could go out and work, gather knowledge, and when they are quite ready, they should come back to their community and open up businesses.

> Leaving a legacy involves more than just money; it
> also requires instilling cultural, social, and civic values
> that will support your community, and give it strength
> and vitality.

Q: So you are training. How did your nursing training help you become…I saw a study somewhere that said a lot of nurses become businesspeople, entrepreneurs. Why is that the case?

A: Because of the leadership skills. As a nurse, as a nurse in charge, there is a lot of time when there is a judgment call, and you have to take care and make certain decisions. So you also interact with the patient, their family. You also interact with co-workers. We also follow rules very well. As nurses, there are certain guidelines you have to stick to. And the discipline of being a nurse helps you. Because these are also some of the things that are required in doing your own business—long hours, being able to resolve issues with your staff or the customer. And so being a nurse, a charge nurse, helps you to do that in your own business.

Q: What made you choose a franchise business, a fast food franchise?

A: I chose a franchise because starting something of my own, I wasn't so confident in myself. But starting something that had a history and having a backup and a support system, that was more logical to me.

Q: You financed the initial franchise with a home equity loan?

A: Yes. When I came to this country, I was living with my mother-in-law and when I moved out of her house, I moved into my own house. I lived there for a while and then I moved to another house. My husband wanted to sell the first one since we wouldn't be living in it—it was a two-family house—but I wanted to keep it, even though it was a struggle. I had to work very hard sometimes when I had no tenant in the house, but I kept it and got equity out of it to purchase my second one-family home.

> Home equity loans are the quickest and least
> expensive method to finance a start-up.

When I decided to get the proceeds and thought about getting the business, I tried getting small business loans. They were telling me about small business development, as a minority, there was money there if your credit was good. There's a way—if you get the right business plan, and the right business, there are funds available. After navigating it tirelessly, I realized that it was not that easy, so

I decided that I would check out the equity in my house, which I had, so I pulled the equity out of my house and I purchased my first business.

Planning and Managing the Business

Q: When you started your first business, did you develop a very formalized business plan?

A: No, I didn't. I just stepped out on faith, and I just thought that if I work hard and learned the business well and take care of the business, it would be OK. But, no, I didn't have an extensive, sophisticated business plan.

Q: You were a nurse, so what kind of skills did you have as a businessperson? Did you understand financial statements, accounting issues? If you didn't understand, how did you acquire those skills or get knowledge enough to feel comfortable in dealing with those issues?

A: I had gotten myself an accountant, and whatever he was doing, I would ask questions. I learned a lot through having the business. So I did not understand what a financial statement was. Golden Crust does provide financial training classes, but I had hired an accountant to take care of the financial part of the business.

Q: Aren't you selling yourself short? Didn't you go to school and take continuing classes?

A: Oh yes, over the time period that I had my business, whenever they were giving classes at York College, anything to do with small business, whether it had to do with tax or whatever, small business, I would go. I would take the time to go and learn.

Q: So you own three franchises now.

A: Right. I have three Golden Crust franchises right now.

Q: What led you to expand from one to two to three?

A: It was a period of time that I had gotten very comfortable. I knew what I needed to know, very comfortable with running the business, and I thought about other family members that I wanted to get involved in the business. So I expanded, and took money from one of the locations, the proceeds I made from the first store after paying back the bank for the home equity line of credit that I had gotten, I took the proceeds from that first store and then expanded, opening the second store. In the second store, I put my nephew as the manager, my daughter as the manager, got them involved and it was doing pretty good, and so I expanded. It was a community in Coney Island. At the time I was working as a visiting nurse and they kept asking me, "When are you going to bring a Golden Crust here? Because we are not close to Flatbush. We're not close to the ethnic area, the Caribbean area." And then I decided that, OK, I'll put one in Coney Island.

Q: Right. And you are running three Golden Crusts now. You've been in business how long?

A: Ten years.

Overcoming Obstacles

Q: What would you say are the biggest mistakes that you've made—your major learning experiences?

A: Not owning the property that I am doing business in. Not being the owner of the store is one thing that I'm learning. Another is not being there all the time.

Q: What are some headaches of running the Golden Crust?

A: People calling in sick. Your cook decides that they don't want to work for you anymore, and you may have to run there and try to make sure that you have breakfast for your customers, and do what you can so the business will function, because even though the cook doesn't come to work, that doesn't mean you are going to close your door. You have to step up to the challenge, and so that was one thing that was good for me—choosing Golden Crust and the Caribbean food, because I had an idea how to prepare some of this stuff. And I would step right in there and go bake patties if I have to, or go ahead and cook some stuff if I have to, mop the floor if I have to.

Q: You mentioned something about family. Your family members are running the other Golden Crust. A lot of people in business say that family and business don't mix.

A: Yeah, some of that, not all of that is true. My family is very loyal and very dedicated to me. They have the same drive that I have and they have the same understanding of achieving that I have. And so it's been pretty good with my family. They are very business oriented. They make a lot of sacrifices, just as much as I've made, so I owe my success also to their dedication.

Q: So you said your biggest mistake was not owning the land of the store. What are some of the other mistakes?

A: That's pretty much it. Not always being there.

Diversified Interests

Q: You are a multidimensional person; you do a lot of things. While you were doing the Golden Crust you also engaged in other endeavors that were not successful. I think you tried to do another business and you lost money in that?

A: Right. I realized the importance of real estate, and so I had gone and purchased an eight-family building in Bed-Sty because I had tenants, but I didn't have a managing agent and I was trying to do it on my own. I wasn't able to manage, so I had to sell that at a loss.

Q: You lost a significant amount of money, is that right? So my question is—we think about the glory of success, but not about the agony of defeat—when you made this mistake, how did you recover? Were you depressed? Did you feel like just giving up?

A: I absolutely felt defeated. I felt like I had failed because this was a property that I wanted to renovate and make this community more beautiful. I also was hoping that this would be a part of my retirement plan. And so when I tried my best with it and wasn't able to hold on to it, yes, I felt defeated. But then I realized that, I also learned a lot. And I took the positive things, a lot of stuff that I learned about real estate and the legal system, where it comes to tenant and landlord, I used it as a positive. I would go out, if I have the money and resources, I would go back and purchase a multi-family building, with the knowledge that I have gathered.

Q: They say in business sometimes you learn more from your mistakes than from your successes. So I guess that experience was a big lesson for you.

A: Absolutely.

Q: I know you are also doing other things. What led you to get into the assisted living business?

A: I always think that you shouldn't put all your eggs in one basket. I do nursing very well, working as a registered nurse. I do that very well. I did the Golden Crust and I did that very well. But I also thought about something different. What if Golden Crust didn't work out? I would have a backup. And being a nurse, I do like working with geriatrics, the elderly. That's something I like to do. So I thought, why not go into assisted living, where you get a chance to have hands-on caring for the elderly. I mean, many of these are citizens who have worked very hard during their lifetime when they were younger and now they are in their twilight years, and I wanted to be involved with that—helping somebody to retire, and know they are not well, and they need someone to take care of them. They would have a nice living center and good care, love and affection, respect, and that is what led me to it.

Q: You weren't motivated by money or profit?

A: Yeah. Absolutely. I would love to make money, but it's not the money so much that pushed me. I took care of my mother for 15 years. My mother lived in my home. I have pictures taking care of her, interacting with her, and I thought about having a place for the elderly.

Q: Do you ever feel overextended, overwhelmed by juggling all your businesses, your real estate?

A: No. I try to be organized and keep my ducks in a row. No, not yet. I also have family that backs me up. I couldn't do this on my own without the friends and relatives, families that are involved. And most of my people have been very loyal. My friends, very loyal. And whenever I'm involved in any project and they see that I'm serious, they would dive in to help me, which I appreciate a great deal.

Looking Toward The Future

Q: OK, superwoman. What are your future goals? What are your future challenges?

A: It is to one day relax, and if my children and my niece and nephew are up to the challenge, to turn over the reins to them and get a chance to relax and enjoy some of the fruits of my labor. I would love to be able to go back to the Caribbean and relax and enjoy the weather, the ocean, and just chill, and retire.

Q: You came to America with just your suitcase. You told me you had the suitcase in one hand, your baby on your arm. We're not going to be here forever. We all must pass on. How do you see yourself building generational wealth? I think that is an important issue for black people too.

A: Absolutely. I think that it is very, very important, and it's one of the things that I'm not just…my children and my nieces and my nephew, they are not just observing me running businesses, or acquiring businesses, but they are also involved in it, and I would like to prepare them and have them one day pick up the reins. And I am encouraging them to learn the importance of owning property, and encouraging them and telling them of the importance of having businesses in their community.

Q: Do you have anything going in terms of retirement benefits for your employees, to empower them for their future?

A: Absolutely. We have. I am working with a bank and we are doing healthcare for them, like HealthPlus, and we're doing retirement benefits. We're working with one of the local banks, HSBC, where that is concerned.

Q: Is that a Golden Crust program or is this something you are doing as an individual?

A: Well, it's a Golden Crust program. They brought it to our attention. They were the first ones who brought it to our attention.

Advice For New Entrepreneurs

Q: What advice would you give to an upstart—someone who just wants to start a business?

A: What I would say to them is: Do your research. Find out if it is something that they absolutely have the knowledge about, and I would also tell them to get their finances together. And I would also encourage them to work in that area, get to understand the area. Maybe they have to work, maybe they give their labor for free. You know, learning the ins and outs of the business, and absolutely go for it. It may not be easy—it's going to be a challenge—but you have to be willing to put all of you into it.

Q: Do you think women face more challenges in business and, if so, how?

A: Yes, I feel that women face more challenges. A lot of times you don't get the respect you deserve to have from some of the old male employees. Sometimes you have to have people coming to work whether it's for repairs, or most of these disciplines, they're male. And they will overcharge you, or don't give you the respect you deserve. But overall, I find that the males in our community are pretty good. They are very supportive and they are always there to give a helping hand.

Q: Let me ask you another question. What business and professional organizations are you active in?

A: It's the BWA, the black business association, black entrepreneur association, black woman business association. I'm a member of that.

Q: I know you are very active in charitable causes and different community issues. Does any of your goodwill—your giving—impact your bottom line? Does it help you in terms of your business making more money?

A: Yeah. In the community I would get involved with the churches and schools, and I would provide funds and sometimes proceeds in the form of food. Many times it has opened a door where there are some other ethnic groups who have not experienced the food that I would give for free, the charitable stuff. They would come back to the store to purchase stuff, saying, "I tasted this for the first time and I like it and now I am coming to purchase it." So a lot of time, I have given a lot of stuff away and it helps to bring people into the store.

Q: So, as we conclude, is there anything else you would like to add or say? Any historical notes or anything else?

A: I just wanted to say that, as people of color, we have to make an effort to purchase from one another, buy from one another. We're not doing enough of that. I hear a lot of call for, we need to open up more businesses and we need to control our community. But I think that we also have to be vigilant and put the word out there, saying that we must buy black—that's one other thing I would say to my children, try your darnedest to support black businesses because if you don't support them, they won't stay around.

I have said the same thing to my colleagues, and some of them have said to me, "Oh, but you know sometimes I've gone to the black businesses and they are not so courteous and they are not so kind and the service was not so good." And I would say to them, "Don't pass an indictment on all black businesses, because I'm sure you have gone to other businesses where the service wasn't so good, and you forgive them and you go back. Why are you so hard on your own people?" So if I go to a business and the service is not so good, I'll go to the manager and speak to them. Or I'll find another black business to go to. But I always make an effort to support my people.

Q: Right. Thank you very much for your time; I appreciate the interview.

SUMMARY

Dawn Bennett's remarkable journey began with her immigration to the United States with nothing more than a suitcase in one hand and a baby on her arm. Now, ten years later, she owns three fast food franchises in the New York metropolitan area, and an assisted living facility for the elderly in Maryland. Her key to success was her dogged determination to succeed, which she supported by working hard and saving her money so she could self-finance her business.

Like many self-made entrepreneurs, Dawn generously gives her time and resources to help others achieve their entrepreneurial goals, and although her humanitarian efforts don't always provide a financial return, she benefits by contributing to her community's future sustainability.

CASE STUDY 8: JOSE ALMANZAR

INTRODUCTION

Jose Almanzar is a young music industry entrepreneur. Although still in his early thirties, Jose has pursued music projects for almost twenty years. Starting out as a break dancer, he has been a singer, recording engineer, producer, etc. He is presently focusing on a recording studio and developing music scores for independent films.

Although Jose has not made a major breakthrough yet, his interview is hopefully inspirational for young people, particularly minority youth, who have big musical dreams. In every borough of New York and throughout American inner cities, there are thousands of faltering music studios recording hip hop and rhythm and blues. His commitment, professionalism, and lessons learned will hopefully serve as a guide to action.

THE INTERVIEW

Background/History

Q: Jose, how did you get into the entertainment music field? What was your first entrée into this arena?

A: When I was about thirteen, fourteen years old, I used to be a break dancer—I started break dancing because I was a gymnast before that—and I met with up with a lot of different people in the hip hop field. A guy named Domingo Padilla, who is a producer now. He has done stuff for Big Fat Joe, Big Pun,

KRS-1, and I met with Tomax, who was a club singer. He used to sing a song called "Regrets Only." So between those two and a friend of mine named Jose who's a musician, they pushed me into taking music beyond break dancing.

Q: And what happened next? After you quit break dancing, what did you do next?

A: I became part of Domingo's entourage. That's when I started seeing the music industry how it is. Being a study with him with Fat Joe, hanging out with Big Pun, Miami, and Fat Joe, and hanging out with KRS-1, just meeting them on a personal level, I started to like the feeling of being around celebrities.

Q: So what made you go from being a performer into the business side?

A: Because after performing for a while, you get tired of it, or you want more. And that's what I was aiming towards. I am a person that…I'm an artist— I went to school for art, and I'm also presently in school for music. So I am always being creative. That's why I do so many different things.

Q: The question was, what led you to go from being just strictly a performer to going into the business side of entertainment?

A: Wanting more. Wanting more. From doing the hip hop thing and the break dancing, I wanted to do more. I wanted to venture out into other aspects of the music field. I became part of the entourage with Domingo and started travel- ing with him and I started finding out that the music industry was more than just performing. Watching him as a producer, I started seeing all the things that he was doing, all the people he was meeting, all the people that he produced stuff for, and just in general, being around the celebrities.

It was just fascinating for me to see what directions they wanted to go—they also wanted to live their lives as performers. So every time I was around them, it wasn't just being in an entourage with Domingo, I was also analyzing the artists themselves. And I was saying, what do they have that I want? Or what do they have that I don't have, besides money and fame?

Q: Who were some of your biggest inspirations? You mentioned a couple of guys. Domingo and somebody else.

A: Well, Domingo Padilla is one—I've had four inspirations from when I first started. Domingo is one and another is Jose. He's a classically-trained guitar- ist, went to school for music, has a bachelor's degree in music, and I learned a lot of music stuff through him because we were in a church choir together. That was one of my other things that I really liked, being in a church choir. That was one of the things that pushed me into the music also.

Another is Tomax. He's a movie writer/singer. He's actually right now in Hol- lywood working on some films and trying to get a major film out there, which is in the works right now. And also David, my engineer. He helps me out because he is patient with me, and I'm a very hard person to work with because I want perfection. That's just the way I've always been. If I want to do something, I want perfection. He's been there, with pay and without pay, he's been there a lot for me, and I appreciate that a lot. So those are basically my four big inspirations in the music business right now.

Q: Do you model yourself after somebody in terms of what you are trying to accomplish from the business side, i.e., Puff Daddy, Dr. Dre, or anybody like that?

A: Basically Dr. Dre. I model myself according to a couple of them because all of them have different parts that I model myself to. Like Dr. Dre, I love his ambition in music. I love the way he goes about, where he is creative, and just what he did with M&M and what he did with a lot of other performers. And even though he went through hard times, he didn't let that defeat him. He went on to the next thing and then, from being broke to back to being a millionaire again. So he is one of my inspirations in the sense of being a producer and doing things, and even though things go bad, you can still conquer what you have to do in life.

Also, Puff Daddy. Puff Daddy because he is just an entrepreneur. I feel like I model myself more towards him because he does a lot of entrepreneurial things in the sense that he does music, he does fashion—that's how I see myself. I do a lot of things in life right now. I am a musician. I am a producer. I am a recording studio owner. I am a carpenter. I am a good friend. I like to listen to people, and I think that is one of my good traits. That's one of the big things I see in Puffy. I mean, I see myself a lot like him because I'm kind of like following his path—not so much being a millionaire like he is, but I see myself as accomplishing a lot in my life now, even if I don't become a millionaire.

Q: What about the people you started with back in the days of break dancing—did many of them fall by the wayside? Have they become successful or given up? Where are they now?

A: Well, a lot of them have families now and a lot of them are not even into the music. One still dances—one of my former partners still break dances—he still uprocks and pops and locks and all that. He is still doing that. And most of them just disappeared. I mean, after a while, I went from being a dancer to being in the entourage to being a producer. So I kind of lost touch with everybody. And since I don't have any kids, I don't have a family yet, I went towards the other route, since everyone is doing their thing with their family, I dedicated a lot of time to my business and my music.

On Achieving Success

Q: So, you see so many young people who want to get into the music field. Their dream is music. Why are so many of them not successful?

A: Good question. Well, what I see on an everyday basis is that the reason a lot of them aren't successful is because they dream it but they don't do it. They dream of becoming successful in being a rap artist or an R&B artist, but they do not work hard at it. Back when I used to do music and produce and do what I had to do, we worked hard. We practiced, because I also used to be a singer, and there were times that we rehearsed two or three hours a day. So instead of us playing video games, or us hanging out with the boys, we would be rehearsing. We would be practicing. We would be writing.

> Nothing will bring you closer to success
> than just plain hard work and dedication.

A lot of people want it, but they don't give the effort. I had a session a couple of months ago with a guy that wanted to be a singer; he was trying to launch a record. A record label owner brought him to my attention and he says, "We're going to bring this guy out. We want you to help him out. We want him to start recording with this artist."

I am not going to mention anybody's name, but I thought the guy was experienced. So as soon as he gets into the vocal booth, he's got his blackberry that he typed a couple of rhymes into, in the blackberry. So as he is going through the blackberry, he's not—he did a half-assed job with the lyrics and he didn't know—what—16 bars—he didn't know anything about music. He was just trying to get on. He was a perfect example of wanting the fame but not wanting to work at it. He expected it to be given to him. I couldn't work with him. I couldn't even finish the song, because the song—whatever comes out of my studio I want it to come out right, whether the person can sing or not. I want, on our behalf, for it to come out right. And there wasn't even flowing—it wasn't going down like that.

So he was a perfect example of he wanted something badly but he didn't want to work at it. He just wanted to be down because that's—a lot of time these young kids, they want the fame, they want the fortune, they want the girls. Half the time they are lying. "Oh, I know this person. I know that person." But most of them, they either carry the books for somebody, or move the chair, or maybe they got somebody water. Half the time. Half the time they don't know these people. Me, I can sit down and say I've hung out, sat down with Big Pun, a couple of months before he passed away. I can say I sat down and had dinner, I had breakfast with Fat Joe. I can say these things. Half these people can say it, but a lot of times they're bullshit. Just trying to get a rep, like the song says, 'just trying to get a rep.'

Q: So besides not working hard, what are some of the other reasons they don't make it?

A: Not working hard and not researching the market. Like right now the market is pretty much going toward down south on the hip hop tip. And on the R&B tip, it's going back to the Mariah Careys, the Mary J. Bliges, and too many people want to do things their style, their way. There's nothing wrong with that. But at the same time, the business has changed a lot. It has become more of a business. So if an A&R is sitting in his office saying, "I'm looking for the next Mary J. Blige, or the next Mariah Carey, or the next 50 Cent, or the next Ying Yang Twins," he's got to find something similar to that, with a twist. A lot of these people, they want to create what they want to create and they want to do their own style. They want to do this and they want to do that—just to do it. They need to study the music. They need to study how songs are formatted, and they need to listen to what's out there and then create their own style, because it's like trying to build a house with no foundation. You have the shell but sooner or later the house is going to collapse because there is no foundation in the house.

Q: So tell me, explain, what do you mean by the music business has changed?

A: Well, a lot of it nowadays, it's more—I'm going to break down a couple of genres. Hip hop has changed in the sense that it is not lyrical as much as it used to be back in the '90s, let's say. It's more bubble gum, more—you've got songs like "Laffy Taffy." It's more about having cars and Benzs and going to clubs and going to this and going to that. Back in the days it was more about being in a struggle, you know what I'm saying? You still have rappers that are into struggle and stuff like that, but those are the rappers that aren't making a lot of noise. A rapper like 50 Cent got it started by being a gangsta rapper, so he kind of brought gangsta rapping back to the East Coast again. Then it got watered back down when he came out with his second album, I mean his third album, when he started talking about "Candy Shop," I mean "Window Shopping," and whatever his other songs are. So like on the East Coast side, we have no rep. So nowadays, a lot of down south rappers are really breaking into the business.

You know, the rap industry is a circle. What used to be back in the days, it'll come back around again. Right now down south has the upper edge over the East Coast. And eventually it is going to come back to the East Coast. But right now, they are the ones making noise. They are the ones with the—I'm not saying there's anything wrong with the music, but I grew up from listening to lyricists like KRS-1 and lyricists like Rakim, where they had deep rhymes, and Guru from Ganstar and listening to those rappers with tight rhymes. And then you have— you still have guys like Mos Def, and you have Common Sense, and you have a couple of the rappers now that still have raps that make sense, and then you have other rappers now that aren't making sense. They are still talking about their Benz and their cars and just different stuff. So eventually it is going to come back around, eventually it will come back around where you have to say something.

But don't get me wrong, most of the time, what a lot of these people think, the young rappers, they think, well, my rhymes are going to get me through. Nowadays, it has always been the formula. There's a quick formula to having a successful song. One of the main formulas is having the right hook. You've got to have the right hook. You don't have the right hook, you can say anything in the world, it's not going to happen. Your song is going to go triple wood.

And the next one is, having the right beats, the right music. If your beat is tight, and your hook is tight, that's a formula for a successful song, or for a song that is going to be heard. And a lot of people don't understand that. You have to create a song for everyone, not just for you and your homies. In this market, the market has changed so much, that when you create a song, you have to create it for you, your homies, your homies' kids, and the people in Albuquerque, the people in California, the people in Spain, all over the world. So in other words, what I mean by that is you can't just—you have to be, what's the word, neutral when you are writing your rhymes. You can't just rhyme so one person can understand you. You have to rhyme so everyone can understand it. A perfect example, when 50 Cent made "Go Shorty, It's Your Birthday," all people remember is "Go Shorty, It's Your Birthday." Stuff like that, like a five-year-old can remember, a ten-year-old can remember, not to say that they should be listening to 50 Cent. But you have to create hooks and you have to create stuff that anybody, that your grandmother could listen to and say, oh, that's a good hook. Oh, I understand that, that song.

People get away from that. They have a song out, a couple of months ago, called "Laffy Taffy." A very simple song, very simple beat, but the beat, I'm not saying the song isn't hot, and I'm not taking anything away from the song, because it's very successful. The beat is very simple—not too done up. The hook, very simple, and a lot of these people know about Laffy Taffy, so he did a metaphor on Laffy Taffy. And it became a very successful song. The formula is there, whether the people research it, use it. It's on them.

> Researching the market is just as important in
> the music industry as it is in every other type of
> business. You can't satisfy your customers if you
> don't know what they want.

Q: So R&B is like that too?

A: R&B has changed in the sense of the lyrics. It has a better feel than the hip hop in the sense of how it changed because you still have R&B singers that talk about passion and love and all that, and then you have the R&B singers that just talk about how I want to get a girl in bed, and even though, back in the days, like Marvin Gaye, "Let's Get It On," but even back then, it was tight. The music was tight. The lyrics were tight, and the feel of the music was tight.

Nowadays you listen to an R&B song, it's like a lot of these producers don't take the time in producing original music. A lot of the songs sound the same. A lot of the music sounds the same. Maybe the lyrics might be different, because nowadays when it comes to R&B, the males have to—the standard is Usher. If it's not Usher, or Usher-ish, then they're not feeling it. Female, it's either Mary J. Blige or Mariah Carey. That's it. If it's not Mary J. Blige or Mariah Carey, they're not feeling it. You've got up-and-coming singers like Keisha Cole. Then on the guys' part you have O'Neil. These are future artists. Now longevity, I'm not sure they would have longevity. That's up to the audience and the people to find out if they want to keep listening to the song. I personally like them, but a lot of these artists, they have to stay fresh, like Usher does. Usher stays fresh. Mary J. Blige stays fresh. Mariah Carey reinvented herself, and these are little keys to success.

I tell people, "Always look at the most successful person and then go from there. Don't look at Joe Schmo from the corner that you admire," even though there's nothing wrong with that, but at the same time, if you are reaching for the top, you've got to look out for who's on top. And then you're not going to be a Mary J. Blige or Mariah Carey, so you work from the top and then create your own thing from there.

Q: So all the people you mentioned thus far that influenced you tend to be Hispanic and black. Do you think minorities really have any power in the music industry?

A: Yes and no. They do but they still go through struggles. They still go through a lot of struggles. The world we live in now, there's still a lot of prejudice in this world. And that's something that no matter if people want to close their eyes to it, it's still happening. So it just happens that a lot of people in the entertainment industry are either black or Hispanic, in the hip hop industry or R&B.

Q: You were answering the question whether minorities have any real power in the music industry.

A: Well money is power, first of all. Money and fame is power. But that only goes so far when it comes to minorities. We as a minority, we still have to put up with a lot of prejudice.

Q: We're back again. You said money is power. Fame is power.

A: But I mean as a minority in the music industry you go through a lot. A perfect example, the most perfect example is when I used to have a magazine called *On the Flip Side*. The name of my studio is the Flip Side Studio, but I did also a magazine called *On The Flip Side*. Now, when I did the magazine, I put my name as publisher, Jose F. Elmar. Jose, a good Hispanic name, Jose. Now when I did it as Jose I never got any kind of calls, any big-time calls, any kind of respect from people in the industry. So I said to myself, you know what, let me change it up a little bit. I put J.F. Elmer. Believe it or not, just that little difference made a big difference. And it's kind of messed up, but it's made a big difference. I got calls from everybody, and it was amazing—I said to myself, "Damn, because they know I'm a minority, they never took me serious. Once I changed my name, they thought I was white!" So once I changed my name to J.F., right away, they think I'm white.

Q: Let's come back to this question later. My next questions is: what made you decide to open a recording studio?

A: Well, about six years ago I worked in a recording studio called Nolo Recording, and it fascinated me working in the studio because I met a lot of different celebrities. Also, I got to see the aspect from creating songs, from scratch, and creating commercials, doing voiceovers. So all that stuff fascinated me looking at the industry in a different aspect, the building aspect of it instead of the finished product.

At Nolo Recording, our biggest contract was Sesame Street—we did all the music for Sesame Street. Every single song for Sesame Street came out of the studio. We did commercials for Rita Moreno. That's the lady from West Side Story. We did stuff for her. We did commercials. We did car commercials. So all that stuff fascinated me. But I didn't have any million dollars to spend on a studio. So I started saving money from that time on. I started saving money, buying equipment here and there: spending two thousand, one thousand, every year I would spend maybe five, ten, twenty thousand on equipment. Just buying equipment. It wasn't even put together; I would just buy it.

After I left Nolo Recording, I started doing carpentry. As a carpenter I started making a lot of money. And the money I was making as a carpenter, I would just save up and buy equipment. From buying sequencers, mixing boards, monitors, computers, little by little it started building up, building up. And then the idea came to me. I said, you know what, maybe I can—I would produce music here and there, not for anyone really famous, just for neighborhood kids and just in general for my own satisfaction, just creating beats, just to stay creative in the music industry. At the same time I had my magazine.

So I had my hip hop magazine and then I had my music stuff going on at the same time. But my magazine was presence. I had it first. I was pushing that more, and the magazine could have been very successful. The only problem is, I kept creating instead of trying to get advertisers. So then when I did that, I said to myself, you know what, I need to do the magazine again some day, but I'm not going to do it if I don't have any money. A quick way of making money is creating beats, tracks for singers, artists. So that's when I started putting my two cents together and started creating to design a studio.

Q: What's the name of your studio now?

A: On the Flip Side Studio.

Q: Why a studio rather than a recording label? What's the difference? Why would you do one as opposed to the other?

A: Eventually I am going to do a label, but for now, a studio brings in the money, brings in creativity, and it brings you the people. There could be a time that somebody comes to my studio wanting to do an album and I'd listen to them and they are incredible, and that would be the time when I would create a record label. But until then, I respect everyone that comes into the studio and records, but I go back to the question that you asked me before where I don't see dedication, now in the music, so if there is dedication in the music and if I feel somebody is worthy, not of me, but worthy of me investing in them, that's when I would open a record label.

But the studio right now, I like it all because I get to create. I get to do different things. I'm not just doing hip hop. There are projects that come to us from gospel music to opera music, to commercials, to voiceovers, to cartoons. I mean, that's more of a personality. I like doing a lot of different things. So I guess I took a little bit of my personality and I put it into the studio.

Financing/Managing The Business

Q: So where did you get your start-up money to build your studio and your other activities?

A: Basically by having, at the end of every pay check, by having $5 to $10, enough for about 20 bucks—$10 for a Metro Card and $10 for food and whatever else I had to balance out during the week would come out of a credit card. That's one way. Another way, I would flip the credit cards. I would look for a credit card that had no payments on interest for twelve months, a year. And then I would just—before the year was over I would transfer the credit cards. So a lot of it came back via credit cards and a lot of it came out of my pocket. Working hard. Never sold drugs, never did anything illegal. I just busted my behind and did a lot of side work as a carpenter, a lot of side work. Painting, a lot of work as a carpenter. That's how I got most of my money for the studio.

After a while it just took a toll on me because, trying to create something, that's why I left it alone for awhile, I left the magazine for a while, I just started getting my money together, you know. My credit was OK. I didn't have great credit but I didn't have bad credit. But I didn't want to get stuck with another payment. I had enough payments as it was.

Q: Did you get any financial assistance from your family at all?

A: Nope. My mother's passed away, my father, I don't know where he is, and my stepfather is in Puerto Rico. And I'm the only one in my family that's around, besides my sister.

Q: So when you opened up your studio and you were trying to get financing, did you go through the regular steps of trying to do a business plan and take it to the banks and, if so, what happened?

A: I did. Until this day I'm not finished with my business plan. But I decided to not wait on anybody and just to hustle and make things happen for myself. The way of going about that is: Step 1—I developed a relationship with my engineer, because you have to have the right team around you. That was my first step. Good people to work with. And I developed a good working relationship with him and that was my biggest step.

Step 2: I had to create a studio, so since I was a carpenter the money I was getting from every paycheck, I applied for a Home Depot credit card and I got it and Home Depot had no interest no payment for a year, so I just kept buying stuff and flipping it, you know, and then paying it, and by the time the year was over or the six months was over, that would be paid for. But I would have to do it before they tacked all the interest to it.

Step 3 was having the equipment that I had from buying it previously, and seeing what I needed to make it work. My goal was to have the best studio in Brooklyn that's not worth a million dollars. It's close to, what—50 or 60 to $100,000, but that will give it a million-dollar quality in the studio. That's what my goal is now, and that's what my goal has been from the beginning.

Q: You've described yourself as a creative person, an artist. How did you make the transition? You had the artist skills, how did you make the transition to business skills, like understanding your tax situation, your financials, etc.? How does that affect the creative person?

A: Well, it affects it a lot. Because I have to run a studio, and at the same time I have to be creative in what I put out. Whatever comes in to my studio and whatever comes out of my studio. I worked in a bank and that opened up my eyes to the way businesses are run. Because you're around money all the time, you're around people that know about money, and you're around—lots of time—you're around lots of successful people. So I basically just listened and researched. And when I went back to college I took a couple of business courses. So, planning to me was very essential. Planning, and not listening to negativity.

Those are my two biggest things. Planning what I want to do for the future of my business, and not listening to negative people, because as a minority, I'm sorry, but too many minorities have bad things to say instead of good things to say. People will say, "Why would your business succeed?" So I shun those people. I stay away from them and I only try to be around positive people. The more positive people I'm around, the more creative I am and the more I want to push to go to the next level.

Q: So, you say planning. What do you mean by "planning"?

A: Well, planning is basically research. First of all you've got to say: OK, how much money do I have, and, for the budget that I have, what do I want to do? And then, let's say your budget is $20,000, or $10,000, and for that $10,000 you say: What can I do for $10,000?

A lot of people make the mistake and they plan and they have a budget and they want to do this and they want to do that, and they want it tomorrow, they want it yesterday. Now, my thing was that if I wanted to do the studio, I was going to do it right, and I was going to take my time with it. I was going to look at my pros, my cons, and even though I stayed away from the negative people, I took whatever negativity they said, and if it made sense, I took whatever they said and I wrote it down. Then once I wrote everything down, I said: "OK, they say this is going to fail because of this, how can I counter this to make it work?" So, every time there was a negative, I made it into a positive. I kept on flipping. Everything negative I flipped to be a positive. In the back of my mind, I also knew that things happen, but at the same time I knew how to flip it, because once you take a negative and make it into a positive, you're back into the positives, and you go forward and you take the next step, and the next step, and the next step.

So, with me, as an entrepreneur, what I want to do is be an entrepreneur like famous guys like Puff Daddy or Dr. Dre or even Joe Schmo who made it but maybe isn't such a known name. You know, to make it as a success to me means being happy, not so much because money doesn't mean success. Sometimes people could be happy making a couple of thousand dollars a year and be happy being creative.

Q: Let's say you hit a big contract and next year you do three million dollars. Do you have the business skills to really direct a multimillion-dollar company?

A: Yes.

Q: If you didn't have them, how would you do it?

A: Well, I have a lot experience with management. Because in all my previous jobs I was either a manager, I managed a movie theater where I dealt with millions of dollars a year, or I worked in different companies where I'd deal with a lot of money, and throughout the years I'd take my experiences, I'd take a little experience from every job. And I've always been a leader and not a follower, and that comes in my attitude, in the way I go about things. So three million dollars or whatever would just be a budget that I would have to manipulate and try to make things work.

The first thing I would try to do with something like that is not do what the normal person would do and go buy a car and a house and, you know. The first thing I would do, since I worked in a bank, is I would look for financial advisors. That's the first thing I think any person should do if they ever come across a big contract. In the music industry you hear about a lot of guys that made millions of dollars and are broke. A lot of guys are broke now. Why? Because they never…they used their money, they never used their money wisely. They always used it foolishly. And I would try my best to use it wisely or to flip it the right way, where at the same time I would take my company to the next level but I wouldn't jump too high. Because what happens is, you wind up taking your company from Point A to Point B and C and D without taking the steps. Always take your baby steps.

Q: That's a good point. Let me ask you this: What problems do you have working with other creative people—the artists, the producers?

A: I think the biggest problem I have is vision: You visualize something and they visualize something else, and then when the two visions come together, it can do either of two things: it can crash or it can be a great vision. And that's the problem a lot of people have. The majority of time it crashes. Maybe you see it a certain way and they're not seeing it that way, and then they give you their vision, and you're saying, "What is he, crazy?" But sometimes, because the client is paying, you have to do what the client says. At the same time though, you try not to lose your creativity, because most of the time when they have a vision, you bring out their vision, but then they try to knock your vision and put theirs ahead of yours. You have to try to work between the lines—try to meet in the middle, where you don't compromise so much of your vision, but you don't compromise their vision, because they're the ones that are paying you, or they don't want you being creative with it. And that, I think, is one of the biggest things.

Lessons Learned

Q: So you started break dancing about 16, 17 years ago?

A: No. Over 20 years ago.

Q: Oh, 20 years? So you've been around this business roughly 20 years? What do you see as some of your biggest errors and the biggest mistakes, the best lessons you've learned?

A: In the music, in general? The biggest lessons that I've learned, mistakes that I've made is staying consistent. Consistency is the biggest mistake that I've made. Jumping from one thing to another, whether it be with music or whether it be with art, or whether it be with singing, with anything, just being consistent. You know. And giving up hope: when my mother passed away, I gave up hope and I stopped doing everything. And that brought me down again. And then I went back up and then I started building, taking my baby steps. But I think being consistent is my Number One thing. My Number One thing that I haven't— that I didn't do, that I'm doing now. Because my attitude now, is, This is good, this is it, there's no more second jobs for me. Once this business picks up and becomes more successful, that's it! I'm never going to do anything else. Music is going to be my life.

Q: You're going to college now. Queensboro College.

A: Right.

Q: How is that helping you in terms of your business growth—your music growth?

A: It's kind of difficult because I'm around a lot of younger people, in the sense of, it's good and it's bad. It's good in the sense that they're the main reason why I went back to school. What they are teaching me there I already know; 90% of the things that they're teaching me there I already know. It's bad because sometimes their vision might not be what you're seeing. Because your vision might be a couple of steps ahead of theirs. And they may think, they're taking their little baby steps and you're walking already. But at the same time, on the flip side, I like being around the youth because that's where most of the ideas come from. Listening to them, from being around them, you know, getting ideas from them, and from seeing what they're doing different that I'm not. So that's how I flip the script on that. I try to be around the youth and that's the main reason why I'm back in college. I'm at the point now of being a recording studio owner; I don't need a degree for that! Recording studio owner, you need the money and the right engineer. That's it.

Advice For New Entrepreneurs

Q: So these young people that you go to school with now—what would you tell them if they wanted to get started in the music industry today?

A: I would tell them: Work hard, don't give up, and keep going for whatever you want to do. If you want to be successful at something, go and do it, whether it's hip hop, R&B, engineering, producing, whatever you want to do.

I'm the type of person that, if a person owns a studio, I tell them: "I already helped out three recording studios" because my attitude is, this business is for everyone; you can't hate and hold back information just because somebody else wants to do the same thing you want to do.

Q: You're saying that what you might tell the young people you're going to school with is, "Don't give up; don't quit."

A: Be consistent. That's my main, main, main thing with people. If you know you're not good at something, like let's say you want to be a singer but you can't sing, then write. If you can't write, then produce, or if you can't produce, then arrange. But if you love music, stick with it, and there are many aspects of music that you can flip, you know. Some people want to be a singer; they can't sing, but that's the thing that they want to do. More power to you! But, keep in mind, you're not going to be the next Usher or the next Mariah Carey or Christine Aguilera, Kelly Clarkson, you know. That's what you've got to keep in mind.

There are levels of success and there are levels of talents. Some people could be a horrible singer and become a little bit of success, what's it called "five minutes of fame"?

Q: Fifteen minutes of fame.

A: Fifteen minutes of fame, like William Hung. The boy can't sing to save his life but he sold some records. If you want to be "flavor of the month," that's on you. But you have to keep in mind: be realistic of what you want to do. If you want to produce, produce. If you want to sing, sing. Can't sing? Do something else. Can't produce? Write. Can't write, arrange. But if you love music, find your niche in the music and keep at it, keep at it, be consistent, be consistent, be on top of it. And the main thing I tell people all the time is: don't let things bring you down. Number one thing they are going to encounter in this music industry is people bringing you down, or things bringing you down. Whether it's financially or whether it's someone, a friend of yours saying that "this is no good, this is no good" or "You're not doing this right!" You have to try to have your ears open, but at the same time, shut down a lot of things. Someone tells you this is bad, then you say to yourself, "Why is this bad, and how can I fix it?" Then you try to fix it.

If someone says that you can't sing, then you say to yourself, "Well maybe I can't sing that well; maybe I'll get a singing coach." Then you get a singing coach to train you, and if that doesn't work, then you're back to square one; you start arranging music or start writing.

Q: Here's a question: you keep mentioning all these big mega stars. Isn't it possible that the use of the Internet and then publishing your own songs, promoting yourself, isn't it possible for a singer who may not have the notoriety of a Mariah Carey to still make a lot of money in this industry, still be financially very successful?

A: With technology nowadays, 100% yes. There are many ways of making money in this industry, where you don't have to be at the top of the charts in order to make money. Nowadays with the Internet, with the Ring Tones, with MySpace, all these Internet things, you can make tons of money.

If you have an idea and you market it right and you flip it right and you work hard at it, definitely. The difference is, these guys are out there. We hear about them every day or every other day, and we see how much money they're making in *Forbes Magazine* and, the Average Joe could be successful in scoring a movie and you might hear about it, maybe they're doing 20, 30 movies a year, charging maybe $15 to $20,000 a movie and becoming a millionaire but quietly, you know what I'm saying? On the DL? Very quietly, doing, taking the small steps.

Sometimes people think you have to take big steps in order to succeed. If they take smaller steps, you know, there's a possibility you could become a millionaire! And be successful in this industry.

Looking Toward The Future

Q: So you're still a young man—in your early 30s—what do you see as your future challenges, goals, things you want to achieve?

A: Well, the direction I'm heading towards recently has been with movie contracts and scores. It fascinates me because I can do just about anything with movie soundtracks and scores. Any type of music, I mean. And I want to someday score a major movie: that's my goal, period! Whether I win a Grammy or not, that would be nice—if it happens, it happens. But just scoring a movie, a major movie, that would be great. That would be my dream. If that's the last thing I do in this industry, then I'll be happy.

Q: So you see yourself from working in this recording studio to maybe what you said, if you found an artist with a lot of potential you might do a record label or you might score movies. You sound like Quincy Jones to me.

A: Yeah, you're right. You know what? You're right. Quincy Jones, that's another big influence. I forgot to mention him.

Q: I know you don't have any kids now, but when you do, how do you intend to create generational wealth? How will your kids, the people who are behind you, going to be able to enjoy your success?

A: I think from the variations of styles of music that I create. That and the warmth in my music. And just staying different and staying creative at all times. Even though everyone has a style that you say, OK that's their style, I want people to say, "That's their style but it's a little different this time around." I don't want them to say, "Oh, that sounds like this person"; I want them to say, "That could sound like this person, but it's different."

Q: Right. But what about creating generational wealth for the people who come behind you? I'm assuming that you're going to be financially successful—what are you going to do with the money that you make?

A: I have a few ideas. I do a little bit of real estate because right now real estate is booming, and I want to see if I can invest in a couple of houses—maybe one or two "Handyman Specials"—get involved in fixing them up myself a little bit, and flipping the money. And always keep the real estate thing going. But at the same time invest my money in IRAs, in mutual funds; try to put some retirement money on the side. That way when I'm 62, 63, I don't have to worry about my future, my living.

Also, my main thing is that I want to buy a building for myself and have basically an enterprise in that building—that's been my dream. One of my dreams. Basically, have a recording studio, a dance studio, a recording label, offices for my recording label, and just have it all in one building. I've never seen that in New York. Probably someone has done it before. But I want to buy a building where everything's right there—you don't have to leave. We have our own distribution company, our own recording studio, our own record label, everything in there. So when an artist comes in there, he's coming from beginning to end! He's leaving with a CD in his hands.

Q: In business they call it "vertically integrated," like in South Africa and Liberia, they control the diamonds in the ground to the finished product. Every aspect they control. So, I don't know whether you're old school or new school. Given your age, I think you're somewhere in between.

Now, as we finish up, what last thing would you like to say that could give advice to others, or point out where you're going with your entrepreneurial career? Anything you feel like bringing up?

A: Well, I feel like, to make it easier on people, when you're young, save up money and invest it in long-term CDs. If I knew 10 years ago what I know now I would invest my money into long-term CDs. That way, I know 10 years from now this is the money I have looking forward to.

There are lots of little things that people will give advice about and say, you know, work hard at this. If you work hard at something and you're consistent good things will happen. On the flip side you've also got to save whatever little money you make. By doing that, you're not worrying about the banks. You've got to control your destiny. And if you have a little bit of money, or a lot of money, the control you have in your life is a lot better than what you'd have if you let a bank control your life, in other words, getting a loan, getting your credit. If your credit is bad but you've got money saved up, you don't have to worry about getting a loan.

So that's what I would say: Control your own destiny. If you work at a job, whether it's at McDonald's, in an office, or in a hospital, put money away every week, every week, open up something—a CD where you know you're not going to touch the money, where you know that's your best investment, where you don't have to worry about losing money. And after that certain amount of time, plan: Plan what you want to do in your future. If you have money that you know is coming to you 10 years from now, you say "Wait a minute, I have $10,000 coming to me in this month, this year, what can I do with that money, and how can I take care of my own destination where I don't have to worry about getting a loan from the bank?"

Develop a plan, create it, and within the time that you're waiting, make moves. Always make moves. If you have a business, whether it's a record label, recording studio: research, research. Nowadays you go on the Internet, you get all your research. Go to the library, read up on it—that's what I did most of the time, before I started the studio. I read books on it, I talked to people that owned recording studios. I worked in those studios so I knew more or less how it ran.

And just stay positive. Always stay positive and keep going forward, forward, forward. Tons of obstacles are going to be in your way. You've just got to keep moving forward. It's like a person climbing a hill that's steep. You know, you're always going to have that battle going up, taking steps, every step that you take is hard, but you know you're going to reach the top of the hill. And that's what you have to do. Reach the top of the hill.

Q: Well, thank you very much for the interview.

SUMMARY

Jose Almanzar began his music industry career as a break dancer—turned musician. A man of many talents, Jose has explored different avenues within the music industry, analyzing what successful performers have done, and emulating them to bring his vision to life. He is a firm believer in a strong work ethic—you've got to put forth the effort if you expect to see the desired results.

Jose followed his own recipe for success by working hard, saving his money, and purchasing equipment over time, so when he was ready to open his own recording studio, he was able to finance the endeavor himself. His philosophy about what it takes to achieve your objectives, which he emphasizes to the young people who see him as a role model, is to be consistent, focus on your core competencies, research your market, dedicate yourself to the business, and work hard to get where you want to be.

CASE STUDY 9: ESLEY PORTEOUS

INTRODUCTION

Esley Porteous was born in Jamaica. In his native country, he learned plumbing skills and dropped out of school at the age of fourteen. He came to the U.S. as a migrant farm worker. After arriving in New York, he worked for several plumbing contractors and developed his sprinkler systems expertise.

Currently, his company, Expert Sprinklers, is the most successful minority vendor in this field. He has been somewhat successful in obtaining contracts for a few major development projects, but the company is struggling to improve its management administration capacity and hire more professionals. If successful, Esley maintains that this will lead to a drastic increase in annual revenue.

THE INTERVIEW

Background/History

Q: My first question to you is this: Growing up in Jamaica, was your family involved in business? Were you from a business environment?

A: When I was growing up in Jamaica, we had large properties with a lot of different foods and vegetables. So we just sold our own stuff. We learned to do business from what our family actually did: sell mangoes, sell different stuff. We never saw our family actually really working with anyone—just selling their own produce from the farm.

Q: So would you say your family influenced you to have a kind of business sense?

A: My father used to be a contractor, like a building contractor. So we learned to work with him, and we said, "When we grow up, we want to be the same thing; do what he does." My brothers are all basically contractors right there in the state.

Q: That's important, because research shows that a lot of people who are entrepreneurs get it from their family. Their family influenced them to become entrepreneurs.

A: My mom was a higgler [someone who buys and resells products]. And she used to take us to the market with her, as little kids. So she would have a little bed to the side for us to sleep, for a kid to sleep, and then we would see actually what was going on. So we grew up with that type of business sense from babies, baby stage.

Q: So your family influenced you to go into business, but when you started your business, did your family contribute financially?

A: No, they did not even know that I was starting a business. It was new to them—they had no clue.

Q: This is the same question I asked Dawn Bennett. When you go to the island of Jamaica, you see a lot of Syrians and other people who seem to own all the businesses. But when you see Jamaicans up here, they are very active in business, entrepreneurs and all that. So would you say your experience in Jamaica really influenced you, once you came to America?

A: I came to America the first opportunity I got. My mother didn't have any clue that I was coming here. I came here [to New York] actually. People come to Jamaica and they choose young healthy men. If you are strong and healthy with no illness, they bring you to work on the plantation here in America.

Q: You mean down in Florida?

A: No, wherever they have the plantations, you work there. First when I came here, I was working on the upper plantation, up in a place called La Grange, which is a little way out of Poughkeepsie. So I was working with a company called Cross Heritage. I worked there, picking apples—and you have to be very careful picking the apples, because if you squeeze them, they look in the bags and they say you are bruising the apples, so they tell you to come off the trees, so you have to be very, very careful.

I would pick like five or six bags a day—huge boxes. I did that for approximately four to five weeks, picking apples, until I just ran away.

Q: What did you do next?

A: I left Poughkeepsie and went to Brooklyn, New York, to live with my sister there. I had two pants, two shirts, a leather jacket and my bag when I got to my sister's house. I stayed there and they said they were going to look for a job for me. They kept searching around, but they didn't really find any job until I started selling.

The gentlemen that picked me up from Poughkeepsie, he had a little business going. He had one of those canteens—you sell coffee, pastrami, butter rolls, so he said I could work with him. I was working with him getting about five to ten dollars a week. He kept saying he was training me to operate the business, but apparently he was just having me working.

So I did that, and I told him that I am a plumber. So he said, "If you're a plumber, you could get a plumber's license and you could set up a business," and I said, "Yeah, that's good. Because that's what I used to do in Jamaica. I used to do plumbing; that's my trade. I never did anything else."

He said, OK, but then he never really put what he said into action. So I started searching around for a job. There was a place on 14th Street in Manhattan that had all these employment agencies where you pay about $50 to get a job, so I paid $50 and they sent me to the Bronx. And I interviewed with a guy who said, "Well, yes, we're going to call you," but they never called me. Every day I would go and I put five cents in the phone, calling and saying, "What happened?" They would say, "Call back tomorrow, call back tomorrow."

I told this to somebody else and they said, "Go back to the agency and tell them you want your money back, and go to a different agency and see what you can do." So I did. I went back to the agency but before taking my money back I walked around and saw another agency in the same area. I told them I am looking for a plumbing job and the guy says, "Take this number and go there now, because the man is hiring and he is waiting for you." So I went to the other agency and told them, "Listen, I need my money back because I don't really want to work, just give me my money, my mother will help me out." I was just saying that for them to give me the money back right away. So I got the money and gave it to the other agency, paid them, and they sent me to this job interview on 75th Street and Third Avenue, to work with a plumbing company, which does both sprinkler and plumbing. And I started working with them.

I had to take my tool bag on my back all over the city. We did the four boroughs, not Staten Island, but the four boroughs: Brooklyn, Queens, Manhattan, and Bronx. And I did that for a while until the Fire Department told my boss, "Listen, why don't you give him a letter so he could take the test," and he kept saying yes, but he never did it. So I worked at a different company and a gentleman there gave me a letter so I could go to the Fire Department and take a test to get my inspection license. So I did that. I got my inspection license and in 1992 I started up my business.

Q: How did you get your training in sprinklers?

A: Well, my training in sprinklers was with that company—Acro Sprinkler. I was already a plumber, so it wasn't that hard to pick up sprinklers because it's the same pipe work. The only difference is that you're dealing with…like in plumbing you'll be dealing with toilets and drains. In sprinklers, you are just dealing with risers and branch lines and sprinkler heads and alarm valves and different components that work along with sprinklers.

Q: So you started your business in 1992; why did you decide to start it then?

A: As I said, I was working with this man, and at the time he was spending very small. And I was very loyal. I would always be at work by seven o'clock in the morning, never late, never absent a date. Every day I'm at work, seven o'clock, sometimes I work at night at his house doing repairs, doing little stuff for him. And on Saturday I would work too. Well, the man was getting real old, and so during the time I was working for him, somebody asked me if I wanted to be a superintendent.

I was thinking, the money I was getting from him wasn't enough to sustain myself and my family and to pay rent, so I thought, if I get a superintendent job, it will help me to be able to sustain my family better. So I got the job. And it was paying me a little more than what he was paying me. But I just told him that I was helping my sister out; I didn't tell him I got the job until I was settled into it. Then I went back to him and told him, "Thank you for the time I worked with you, but I found something a little better and I am going to move on." He wished me luck and I said, "Thank you very much," and I left in good faith.

Q: When you started your business, where did you get the start-up money?

A: Well, actually, I didn't have any start-up money. First, there were some people out there that you could pay $50 a month, I think, for an answering service. You didn't have cellular phones back then; you had beepers. So you would give the answering service your company name and beeper number and if somebody called for a job, they would beep me. Then I would call them and they would tell me where to go. So you could call 24 hours a day and you would get somebody answering, "Expert Sprinkler, may I help you?"

Q: So when you first started, did you work with anybody else? Was it you and a couple of other guys?

A: Just me. Just me. And I believed in myself.

Q: Were you making any money doing this work—was it worth your while?

A: It was worth my while because it was sustaining me. I was living from it, taking care of myself, and taking care of a lot of other people. So it was fine for me.

Q: So you were pretty much like a subcontractor when you first started?

A: I wasn't actually a subcontractor. I was just working for anybody. A lot of people knew me from way back, and the old man [previous employer] had also passed away.

Q: You had a company called Expert Sprinkler. If they wanted you, would they pay Expert Sprinkler, or would you just go work as an individual?

A: I would go and do the work and they would make out the check to Expert Sprinkler. I was a sole proprietor for Expert Sprinkler. I became a corporation in 1996.

Managing The Business

Q: In reading the different books, particularly about the big MBA people, before they jump into business they have this elaborate business plan. When you started, what did you start with? What kind of planning did you do?

A: That is a very funny question. To be honest with you, it was just something that I was always doing—before I came to America I was also doing my own business back home as a plumber. I opened my own business named Esley Plumbing Service, going around all over the island working for different individuals that required my service.

I just believed in myself, knowing that if you could produce a service that the public requires, you are always going to have somebody to call you. Once you know what you're doing and you do a good job, the word is going to go around, and it just keeps going and going until you have to hire help because you get so much established, you cannot handle the workload by yourself. And that's just my plan. Keep doing it.

> Find a need in the marketplace and fill it. If you're
> providing a valuable service and you do a good
> job, you *will* build a profitable business.

Q: Of all the people I've interviewed so far, nobody started out with a formal business plan. So I'm not surprised that you didn't have a formal business plan.

A: It's just what was in my head. I didn't write out anything. It's just in my head. And I'm still having different things in my head, but it's like I'm being defeated by different organizations because when I popped up and people heard about Expert Sprinkler, they weren't even looking to see me as Expert Sprinkler—a lot of people don't know who Expert Sprinkler is. A few people might know, but they don't really know. If they saw me out there, they would know, he owns Expert Sprinkler, or he is the owner of Expert Sprinkler. They would know.

Q: Reggie Lewis, who is the richest black business owner—he owns a billion dollar company—and when he was building this company it was five or six years before anybody knew he was the owner, that a black guy was the owner because he always sent a white guy, his assistant, to negotiate the contract or to represent the company.

A: We ourselves don't respect ourselves. It's frightening.

Q: So you had the contracting skill—how to do all the plumbing and all that. What were you lacking in terms of business skills when you first got started? What were you really lacking?

A: Well, I know the mechanical aspect of the business and I know also how to interact with clientele as far as selling my skill and my know-how to make somebody feel satisfied with my work. What I was lacking was the administration part, like when I go out there and work and someone to really follow up with collecting and stuff like that.

Q: The administrative aspect. So how long—how many years—were you working basically by yourself?

A: Well I started like that, and what I would do at the end of the day was, I would take everything home and then my wife and I would get the bills together and I would send the bills to the different clientele. Finally my workload was getting so large—the answering service people were calling me so much that I decided to open an office, so I got a little basement place on 96th Street and Central Park, between Central Park and Columbus. I employed a young lady who was very, very young, but she had some business background, so she would run the office. She would take messages. She did that part of the business.

Q: They say that during the first three or four years, most businesses lose money. If a person is lucky, they break even. So in your first three or four years, what were you doing—breaking even, losing money?

A: Well, to be honest, in my first couple of years, I was doing much better because I was actually there doing the work and I didn't have many people who were not producing the actual work—I was doing the work. I was able to keep up with my staff, with everything, until things started to expand—getting more workers, and then it started getting out of hand, especially working with unions.

Q: So for the first few years of your business, what were the basic mistakes you felt you made, the basic lessons that you learned that somebody else could learn from you?

A: The first lesson I learned is that you've got to make sure you keep up with your taxes, and also, you cannot put friends in business. If you try to help a friend, probably the friend says, "OK, Esley is my friend, so Esley is going to help me." But he's not thinking, "Well, he's trying to make a business grow so we could all be happy." He's just there to take, not to put anything there. Nothing. And those are the things that you have to look out for in business. If you could keep those away from your business, the sky is the limit.

Q: One of the people I interviewed has a successful restaurant. She mentioned the same point that you mentioned. She said she had to fire her own mother because her mother wasn't doing the work. I mean, it really validates your point.

A: Yeah, even my son, who I am trying to bring up in the business—he went to college and that didn't work out, then he tried to learn a trade—to work within this business, so he could be the next person to take charge, but it's like he's not really seeing it. But I am still not giving up on him; he's only 22.

Q: What was a significant event for you that took you from one level to the next level, when you got your first contract or something that put you into a different position?

A: I would say, my first contract that took me to a different level was with Macys in downtown Brooklyn. I think at the time it was just changing over from A&S to Macys. Our contract was to do a sprinkler system, and the union was involved, so it was like, I would have to go to the union hall to tell them who I am and everything else, so they say, "Welcome to the real world," because that's my first union job.

Q: What year was that?

A: That was '96, if I'm not mistaken, '95 or '96.

Q: And did you get this work because you were a certified minority vendor?

A: No. I got the job because I was a noted contractor that was doing the general contracting work as far as the dry wall and stuff, and I'd done small jobs for him, so he pulled me on the job and I was licensed and everything to do it.

Q: Have you gotten a lot of work because of being a certified minority contractor?

A: No, I don't get a lot of work from that; I just get work in general. A lot of people come to me because they check around and they find out that I'm one of the only minority sprinkler guys and they check around and they push work my way, send jobs, but sometimes it doesn't work out because different things are involved and they just don't give you the right price. They want you to do it as a minority contractor but for the lowest, lowest, lowest price, like you are doing the job for nothing. So for a lot of people, it doesn't make sense to put your name out there as a minority contractor because it's like they say, "Well, OK, come and take the job. You have to take it for less than the market value, and you have to do twice as much on the job." And I've proven myself. I take it and I do twice as much and it's a lot of problems.

Q: That was kind of my next question. What were your experiences in working with some of these bigger contracts? I know you worked on movie studios, contracts in Brooklyn, and you did some work for York College. What were some of your experiences as a certified minority vendor?

A: First thing, if you are not in a certain clique, and you don't know how to—I don't want to use this term, but it's like you have to actually go around and kiss ass, and I don't know how to do that because I was never brought up in that way. I know how to respect and be humble, and to understand, but as far as to work and then kiss somebody's ass, I just don't know how to play that part of the game.

> Working on government projects isn't
> always the "dream job" that some might
> think it is. Rely on yourself first.

Q: So would you say that a lot of big openings for minority contractors, is it a negative, is it positive?

A: It's a negative to me because the way I see it, I just finished…I just did a job in Brooklyn that was a minority set-aside, Medgar Evers College.

Q: Yeah, I know their project.

A: And we did a very good job on the sprinkler. But until this day, we have still not finished getting paid. And it's just a problem. And they tried everything to discredit us on the job. Even guys that don't know what they're saying, they probably have a degree, they say they're engineers, but they actually know only the basics of the trade. They just walk around and because we are minority contractors, they try to push you, and then if they make a mistake, they're not man enough to come and say, "Well, you know, it was my mistake." They were right. Stuff like that. We encountered it. We get the hardest part of the job for less money too.

Q: That was one of the reasons I wanted to interview you, because as one of the minority contractors, you have a lot of potential in terms of what you do.

A: Because I did a lot of jobs at Columbia University, I was doing very good at Columbia University. We did jobs that many huge contractors wouldn't do because we'd do things like cut pipe and put it together, and people would say, "Oh, you got to rip the hole at this time," and because we are trying to prove ourselves, that we could do the work in any situation, we did it, and after we pulled through, we had people go and sabotage our work. They sabotaged a job for me at Columbia University and it cost my insurance company $78,000, plus it cost me from my pocket another $20,000. I did not get my money back. I had to put it out of my pocket. And then it took six to seven months to get the small little portion of money they had left for me.

Q: So what are some of the problems you have with primary contractors, because I know while working for Columbia, you probably were working for a primary contactor. What are some of the problems that you have?

A: They don't want to pay. They want you to supply all of the materials, all the union labor, and when you put in a requisition, they tell you, "Oh, you gotta wait two months, three months, four months."

You know, we did a job, we did the library and the architectural building in Columbia, and when we did that job, they said the elevator wasn't working, so we had to lug all the pipes up the stairway to complete the job. And when we reminded the person in charge of the job they said, "Oh, Esley, you're not union, so all the trades are gonna stop," and I had to get out of the job; they wouldn't work. So I went to the union, and I'm a licensed contractor, and I asked, "What's happening?" So they said, "Esley, if you want to join, we'll put you in but it's gonna cost you $10,000." So I put in for me and one of my foremen—I paid the $10,000 for me and the lead man and they gave me a work agreement for four other men to work on the site, to complete the project. And the contractor did not give me a penny for months. It was another gentleman that finally helped me get paid.

Q: Someone at Columbia?

A: Yeah, at Columbia University. He was saying, "What are you all trying to do—ruin a minority contractor? To put him out of business?" And then they cut me a check for like $63,000; that was the first check after we almost completed the whole job.

Q: Most minority contractors, the reason they can't get into places like Columbia is that they have issues with bonding, insurance, etc. How were you able to get all that together: your bonding, your insurance, your financial statements?

A: Well, I had to have certified accountants. Plus over the years, by working, I was able to get myself a building in Harlem, so, you know, I have a little financial stability, because when you start looking for bonding, first you've gotta tell them your assets! You have to be able to have something that they could take from you if you don't comply. So I was able to get bonding.

Insurance I was able to get because of my knowledge; first when you start off in the sprinkler business, they have to interview you, if you have any basic knowledge of what you have decided to do. So I go through that and I was able to have my insurance and continue with it. It's paid. It's a struggle but I try to keep up with it.

Q: You mentioned [outside this interview] that the Columbia project is a 15-year project, a 30-year project. You also mentioned Medgar Evers College. What do you see are some of the emerging opportunities for minority contractors here in the city?

A: It's very, very, very weak. It's all a hoax. There's nothing strong—it's like they are trying to beat them down. I could tell a few minority contractors, "Well, OK, they might push you, but the only way they're gonna push you is if they have somebody like me behind them to tell them, 'Listen—don't step here. Don't do this. Do this. Do this in order to pull through.'"

I've already been there so I know! So I would probably have to guide them, be a guidance for them, to tell them, "These are the down spots."

And you have to keep your paperwork straight; make sure whatever you do is on paper, because that's how they play with minority contractors—with paperwork, you know. You have to have your engineer, your field guy, and you all have to work together, because they easily could penetrate minority business, easily by turning the guys that work for you against you.

Q: I've tried to assist many minority contractors to take advantage of major economic development projects as certified vendors and I've come to the conclusion that a lot of them are just jokes, I mean they pay a lot of lip service to: "Oh, you can get these contracts," but when we sit down and try to do it with them, it's a whole different story.

A: As far as I'm concerned, I'm one minority contractor that takes a challenge out here—does some of the things that I don't know if most minority contractors do. I'll put myself, like you see right here: around on the wall. I've tried all the different organizations, become certified by the State, by the Department of Defense, you name it, become a part of the union, you name it. You know, keep going, and put my own brothers and them in the union, not flesh brothers but brothers, some of them just coming out of jail have no opportunity, so I'll take them off the street, train them, put them in the union, and some of the same brothers then turn. And it still doesn't break me.

Preparing For Growth

Q: So, where you are now, you're still a young man. What do you think is needed to grow your business—to take it to another level?

A: Right now in my business I need cash because I have to struggle collecting money, and I have to keep up the business, to pay the guys that I'm working with. So it's a struggle—take my money from here, from there, juggle, juggle, pay. And sometimes when we do a job and we're supposed to collect, it takes months, weeks. A young lady here has to keep on writing letters.

So if I were to get a good administrative staff and some cash we could take off like a rocket! Like a real rocket, because I know the business, and if each person would just hold up their end, I could take care of them. A friend of mine has a business, he does the same thing but he doesn't have a license, but he has a good staff and he tells me he's doing about 10 million dollars a year.

Q: A contractor?

A: A black contractor—a personal friend of mine.

Q: So you say you need cash. What kind of changes would you need for management or administration?

A: I would need an engineer to work within my organization, because in this business, you need an engineer to work on your staff. You need somebody that knows how to be like an architect, so when you get a job they can draw up the plan.

You also need a field supervisor who will go out there. Someone who is very intellectual in his penmanship and who knows how to reason with people, because that's one of the key factors in the business. You've got to be able to talk, to know what you're doing to administrate the trade so you don't lose money.

It's like, if the guys are out there working and somebody decides to say, "You're supposed to do this," but that wasn't in the contract, you must be able to say, "No, we need a written change order and everything must be on paper and signed by someone and if it doesn't happen, that work will not continue." Because sometimes they'll tell a contractor, "Oh just do this and we'll take care of it" and after the work is done, they'll tell you a different story: "Oh no we didn't approve it, that was just word of mouth." So we don't want that type of business. If you continue with that it's like you're trying to make somebody happy, and their intention is to make you unhappy, because they are not honest. So the only way to get it real is to say: "OK, you want me to do this, yes, I'll do it, but it's gonna cost this much—will you agree to pay this much? And we could renegotiate and come to an agreement before my guy gets started and then we can sign to it." So this is it. It's all keyed together.

Q: Right. So you need an engineer, a field supervisor, and what else do you need? Anything to do with internal office dynamics?

A: Basically, we have an accountant. That's a part of the business. You just make sure the accountant is here on a monthly basis doing the books, like if it's the 10th of the month you write this check and it's all documented, so at the end of the year you know: John Doe gets $15,000 for his administrative work, this one gets this much, and everything is run in an orderly form. And then everything will work perfectly.

Q: If you had all that, more cash, better administration, how much do you think you could gross annually? What kind of revenue could you generate?

A: I could easily generate at least probably 10 to 12 million dollars, because the business is out there, but if you don't have the money to get to the job and move through it, you're doing things from a scary position. For instance, you give me a job and I look it over and give you a written proposal. I say, "OK, this is what the job's gonna cost. I need x amount of money down," and you sign a contract and everything is straight. If you don't have the cash flow to move to the job and to finish the job, then the job keeps going slow, and you know you don't have the manpower because you cannot employ enough people, so you can't really make money like that.

Q: So it seems like it's a vicious circle—robbing Peter to pay Paul. People pay you slowly so you have to pay here, pay there—juggling—and in the meantime you take a hit on your credit. The banks won't loan you any money because you've got credit issues, even though you could show them the work was there and you have assets—I see that all the time.

A: They take out your line of credit because you can't keep up the thing. You expect somebody to pay you. You do a job in good faith. You try to keep up with your workers, but you know if a man works he's got to go home with something at the end of the week. And then you expect they're gonna pay you. You have the insurance that you've got to pay, which is like probably $6,000 a month. Your rent. Your different overhead expenses. And if you're not getting any money coming in, they'll make you out to be a bad person, but you're actually not a bad person. You're just trying and you don't want to give up. A lot of people just give up.

Looking Toward The Future

Q: So you're still a young man. What do you see are your future goals, your future challenges that you want to accomplish?

A: Right now, I love what I do. Expert Sprinkling. Right now, it's not as strong as it was before, but I got so much help that I'm trying to take my time and save up for bills. But if I could get it back the way I want it, I would just make it grow and leave it for generation to generation, because I know I'm not going to be here working all of my life. I could be someplace else and somebody could call me and I could give them all kinds of advice.

Q: You could also be building generational wealth for your kids and your grandkids.

A: Grandkids and other people's kids. Not just my family, because anybody that's part of the company is part of the Expert Sprinkler family—that's where you eat, so where you eat, you have to take care of where you eat.

Q: So a skilled guy who works for you. How much could they make annually?

A: Wow. A skilled guy, it depends, but a normal base, a regular guy like that who works with me can make anywhere from a thousand a week to probably two thousand, three thousand, it depends on the job that we're working. Like if we're working on a union job and the guy works every day plus overtime—some guys are pulling like three thousand or four thousand a week.

Q: If I wasn't so old, maybe I'd try that!

A: There's some serious money out there. Because most of the guys that I train, they're out there pulling in, one guy tells me he's making nine thousand a month. And that guy is just 28 years old.

Q: To do that you have to be in the union, right?

A: Yeah, you've gotta be in the union. And if you're making that in the union and you're a real good workman, you're an asset. If somebody has you around, it pays for them to keep you, because you're an asset, not a liability to them.

Q: Can you get people in the union? I mean if they work for you, can you help them get into the union?

A: Yeah, if I get union jobs, then I say, "I have this project and I have these guys, they work with me. I'm a licensed contractor; I would like to put them in to do my work," then the union will grant you, but the only problem is: I did it before and those guys, after they get the union book they have no loyalty any more—they start acting funny. They don't know that's when you've gotta pull together to keep it strong. The union is strength! You just need to go to work and do an honest day's work, don't try to analyze, just do an honest day's work.

Q: Is there any future for women in your field?

A: Oh, yeah! Women work with me. Women in the union work with me and make something like 80 something dollars an hour, plus you have to give them extra money sometimes. I have had women work with me on more than one occasion.

Q: They go to an apprenticeship program first and then—

A: I don't know what they go through, but probably they already have been in the union. If I have a project, and I need people to work, and they send a female, I cannot discriminate—I have to give her the job and see what she can do. I've had three or four female workers since I've been in business.

Q: You mentioned that you belong to a lot of different organizations—minority contractors, this, that, and the other. Have they ever really helped you in terms of contributing or building your business?

A: No. For instance, I'm a member of the Mechanical Association—NISA, and every year I pay them, but I never hear anything from them, like they're gonna do anything for me. You just go to meetings and you stick out your business card. I think I have more contracts out here without the organization because a lot of contractors call me as a sprinkler guy. Sometimes they are in difficulty and they'll call me, give me the work and they send their men, come and learn from my guys, and then they start. I really don't care. I think I help more people genuinely, more than a lot of these organizations.

Advice For New Entrepreneurs

Q: So, what advice would you give if a new guy came to you, or a new lady, what advice would you give to a start-up contractor today?

A: The advice I would give them is to start with a minimum work crew, make sure you complete the project, make sure you get paid, and make sure the guys do their work. Because you have guys out there and for the day they don't do anything, and they expect at the end of the week to get paid. And that will pull you right down the hill. And you've got to be social with your worker, but at the same time you've got to be firm. If you're not firm with them, they all take it as a joke.

Q: You've been doing this since '92 and you have almost fifteen years under your belt; is there any other advice you would give people who want to go in business or who want to become a contractor? Anything else you would like to add to that?

A: One thing I would like to add to it, if you are going into business and you're looking for long-term, you should try to get your own place, like try to get a loan from a bank so while you're working you're paying for that building and you know you're going to be long-term. I would not advise most people to try to rent, especially in New York. It's not the best of things. It is not an easy thing.

Q: I'd like to thank you for your interview; it was very fascinating.

SUMMARY

Esley Porteous shared the same entrepreneurial path that many immigrants to the United States traveled—doing manual labor at the outset until he could work his way into jobs that valued him as the skilled tradesman he was in his native country. With hard work, long hours, and dedication to his business, he has grown his company from the one-man operation it was in the early 1990s to the multimillion-dollar-a-year organization that it is today.

Esley followed all the steps that many start-ups are encouraged to take—registering as a certified minority business, joining trade associations and minority business organizations, and working on union and government contracts, and he is preparing to take his company to the next level. Once he has put into place his growth management strategies, Esley's company will become a stronger player in the field of much larger, more lucrative contracts.

CASE STUDY 10: JUAN VARGAS

INTRODUCTION

Juan Vargas is a 28-year-old businessman. Approximately three years ago, he and his brother (who is now 26) formed Vargas International LLC. They started out by importing feminine hygiene products from the Dominican Republic. Their family operated a discount store there, so the brothers grew up in a dynamic business environment.

After successfully building up a clientele for the imported product, the brothers decided to manufacture locally. Utilizing their own money and obtaining bank financing, they established a production and distribution facility. Their product is in over 100 New York-area stores and they are consciously building a brand name and network of selling agents.

THE INTERVIEW

Background/History

Q: Your family has a history of entrepreneurship and being in business, right? Could you elaborate on that a little bit?

A: They've just had different types of businesses. One of my uncles has a mechanic's shop and my father has always had his own businesses, recently it has been discount stores, but he has always been involved in some type of business, and we have just always been around that. So I guess your mentality is a little bit different when you see that.

Q: So how did that affect you—you were saying you learned about accounting?

A: Not so much that you learn about it, it's just that you see it. You see that it exists, and as far as an employee or someone in an employee's state of mind and the way they are, they don't really see the business aspect, the fact that the rent has to get paid, the fact that the light bill and all these things—these are things that employees don't generally look at. They are just there for their paycheck and that's it. Nobody looks at the bigger picture, whereas the boss is forced to. And we've always been able to see that.

Q: I know a very successful black businessman. He grew up working in his father's business—a little convenience store, I think. Did you guys grow up working, like sweeping the floors? Did your father involve you actively in his business?

A: Not so much, I mean, we were there. We went weekends and things like that, but it wasn't like we were constantly involved in it.

Q: Are you first-generation Dominican? You are Dominican, right?

A: Yeah, we're Dominican.

Q: So does this entrepreneur tradition go back to the Dominican Republic?

A: Yes, it does. My grandfather had his own businesses as well over there.

Q: All your experience has been in the New York area, right?

A: Yeah, pretty much. That's where we're at.

Q: And in terms of your business endeavors, how much family support do you get?

A: Well, from our parents we get all the support we need, any support—they are in with us 100%, always. Whatever we come up with, we find a way to convince them that it is a good idea, and they usually jump on the ship and we do it all together. As far as other family members, it's not the same. They don't really share that, I don't know what you would call it, it's just that vision. They don't really share that.

Q: Do you get financial support? Let's say you are starting up your present operation. Do you get like maybe start-up money from your family?

A: From our parents, yeah, whatever they can do to help us, they do. But as far as anybody else, no. Not really.

Q: It's very funny that you mentioned this—I've interviewed about six people before you guys and you're the first ones to say that your family has helped in terms of getting started. Most of the other people's families were doing so poorly that they didn't receive any financial assistance from them.

A: I mean, it's tough. Usually, when you're in the position we're in, from the places we're from, there are not really many resources out there. But you do what you can with what you've got.

Q: So both of you guys went to high school, right? Rather than pursuing a college career, or going to college, you two decided to open your own business?

A: Basically. It was either that or become an employee.

Q: Why did you make that decision rather than trying to go on and get an education, become a professional, etc.?

A: Because it makes you an employee at the end of the day. What is the sense in that? And you just get a head start now. What's four years in school to come out and be well equipped for a job? What's the sense?

Q: Well these books that I mentioned I read about all these MBAs—they went all the way through and got MBAs so they could come out and open their own business—they took a little different route than you guys.

A: I don't know. I've always felt that school, for the most part, was just a waste of time. I always felt like I was able to pick things up—whenever they were teaching anything I was able to pick it up quick. So for me, it was just a waste. It has always been a waste. So I just said, let me just do what I can do. See what I can do.

Q: Studies have shown that most entrepreneurs tend *not* to be highly educated, or formally educated—that they don't go away to college.

A: Because it institutionalizes you, changes your own mind. You can't—if you go through that, you will end up being an employee most of the time. That's just the way it's built; it's built to do that.

Q: What made you guys decide on this present business? Did you have any other businesses before this one?

A: Before this, no. This is really our first entrepreneurial endeavor. It was the first one we are actually pursuing, big like this, and I think it just came out of an idea, you know, just the idea of getting involved in something like this, getting involved in a product and promoting the product and things like that, and eventually it just shifted. Now we have our own product that we're pushing and that's just what it is.

Q: How did you and your brother decide on the original product you started importing from the Dominican Republic?

A: It was just a product that had a high demand here, so we figured, let's sell it, and we became exclusive, so with the company from the Dominican Republic, we were the only ones allowed to bring it in and it had a high demand, so we were able to do that. From there, it was a thing of investing into promotions and advertising for it, because no matter how well it's doing, it's never enough. So instead of pouring in investments into somebody else's brand, we just created our own.

Q: How did you choose that product and get exclusive rights to it? What kind of negotiations did you go through to do that?

A: Well, it was back and forth with the manufacturer from the Dominican Republic until eventually it just came down to an exclusive agreement, contractual agreement. It was simple as that. I mean as far as picking a product, to us it was just a product that had a high demand, so it really didn't matter what it was going to be. As long as it sold we were going to get in it. That was that.

Q: Can you describe your product a little bit?

A: Feminine hygiene products, something like Summer's Eve—just feminine washes.

Q: You said you are in 100 stores. How did you go about that? How did you get your first accounts?

A: Well they were already there. Like I said, it was a product that already had a demand. The product was already getting in here, scarcely—it didn't have as much of a feed as we were willing to give it. We were just importing more of it. That's what we were going to do. But basically it already had its demand. It was already available in the stores, so there wasn't much left for us to do. That's why it was as simple as it was.

Q: You mean a similar product was already available?

A: The product that we started distributing, yeah. It was already available. So we didn't really have much to do. There were already distributors involved. There were already people visiting the individual stores, so all we had to do was feed the big guys. And that was it.

Q: Maybe you could explain a little more about feeding the big guys. How did you do that?

A: Just selling in quantity, selling in bulk, and then they would go out and sell it to small accounts.

Q: The reason I ask is that I've had some experiencing selling to big guys like JCPenney and Sears, and I know how hard it is to get to the buyers, the decision makers.

A: Well, not guys like that. They already have accounts with distributors. Those big accounts tend to not deal with manufacturers unless the manufacturer is somebody huge already, as big as them or bigger. But they usually deal with distributors already and they have their list. These distributors were already selling to them and we just started selling to the distributor. We just became a middleman. That was all it was.

Q: So you sold to the distributor? What did that make you officially, like the manufacturer's rep for the people in the Dominican Republic?

A: Pretty much that's what it was. We were their face here, in the United States.

Q: What are the biggest headaches for being in that position?

A: Your expenses are high. So that's always a situation. You have to have a big warehouse, delivery systems, logistical and things like that, which all come with huge costs.

Q: Big inventory costs.

A: That's really the main headache. Every month. Big bills. That's it.

Q: How successful were you? What kind of volume did you build up?

A: Well, we have been doing all right with it, but it just became pointless to us to deal with somebody else's product if we could just sell our own, do the same thing. You know, we were about to invest major money into somebody else's brand. We invested a little bit, and saw that it was giving results, so we just pulled back and said, you know what, let's just invest in our own.

> Don't get too far away from your money—
> invest only in your own projects so that
> you have total control over how much
> money you make.

Q: And how did you develop your own product? Did you go to a different manufacturer?

A: Different manufacturers. You create your own brand and then you come up with a product. It's not too much what the product is or anything like that; it's not really about that. It's more about realizing that you have a product and being able to find a market for that product and marketing it successfully. It's all in the marketing.

Q: So in hindsight, if someone was bringing a product, an international product into the American market, what would you advise them in terms of entry strategy? How would you tell them to get their product on the counters, on the shelves? I mean, are you talking about lower pricing?

A: It all depends on what vision you have for your brand. If you are trying to go for a higher pricing with low quantity levels, then that's one thing. If you want high quantities with low pricing, it's a different level. It all depends on how you want to go about it. But there are plenty of people out there already in the business without the investment dollars, without the balls to do things, who are willing to help you with yours. So it's just about getting out there and finding those people and connecting and making it the right circumstances.

Q: Is your market very saturated?

A: Not really.

Q: It's not really a saturated market.

A: No, but you could do it with anything. If you were going to do floor tiles, for example, or something like that. It all depends. Do you want to deal with selling tiles every single day? Then you would have to sell them for 50 cents a tile. If you want to sell only a few tiles but they're really good tiles, like marble tiles or granite tiles, then you are going to be getting ten dollars for each one. You just have to know where to put it and who to talk with to get it where it needs to be. And there are plenty of people to do that. The Internet is full of them. All you have to do is just realize what it is you want to do and get out there and get the people to help you. But there are plenty of people. As long as there is money involved for anybody, they will be willing to get involved.

Q: The reason I ask is that a friend of mine brought housewares from Spain, like mops, brooms, brushes and all that, and he was competing against China—they can do things cheaply. And he could never compete. He eventually stopped doing it because he could never figure out how best to get into the market and make money out of it. So he eventually just gave up.

A: It's all about creating brand. It takes time and investment, money. A lot of times you give up because of that. If you don't have the bank for it, you can't compete. But, why does a Swiffer sell as opposed to a broom? In essence, it's nothing but a broom, but it's out there. They created a brand name for it. That's it. It's a brand.

Q: Since my friend was Hispanic, he tried to use some of these Hispanic programs that give preference to Hispanic businesspeople and all that. Did you guys go that route?

A: No, not really. There are a lot of things that you can take advantage of with being minority and things like that—a lot of programs available for people if you go that route. But generally I wouldn't say that it will help that much because it has its part where it hurts as well.

Q: It didn't help him.

A: There are ways it can help and ways it can hurt. It all depends. If you want to go that route, you can try, but it's the same if you don't. The mechanism is all the same. You've got to just go with—I don't even know what to say—I guess go with your gut. But wherever you can get funding, do what you can do.

Q: Well my friend had an exclusive with the manufacturer in Spain so he was trying to sell to everything from the 99 Cent Stores to the bigger stores, but he just never made much progress with it.

A: If you are battling on price points with somebody who can go down further than you can, there's no winning that battle. You have to figure out—innovation. A lot of things have to do with that as well. If you are new to a market, if you create a market for a product, your product is new or there is nothing like it out there, it makes it much easier for you. If you are trying to sell something that everybody is selling as well, it's a little harder.

Q: So you're saying your product is more a unique product, a little newer product.

A: I wouldn't really say that. It's got its particular demand and that's all it is.

Managing The Business

Q: How old are you?

A: Twenty-eight years old.

Q: You went to high school and started your own business. How did you and your brother train yourself in business management? How did you learn the basic skills to run a business?

A: We're still learning.

Q: Define 'learning.'

A: Well, a lot of it is just common sense. There's not really much to it. The basics. You need a phone. You need all these resources that you need in order to conduct any type of business in order to do anything. Those are all logical. And then from there, what exactly else would you need? To know how to be able to manage all these things? I guess it's just common sense.

Q: What about financial statements, IRS, how to deal with your taxes and all that?

A: It's like I'm saying. If you get the right people involved, you don't really have much to worry about. We are lucky enough to have a good accounting firm. They deal with a lot of big accounts and for some reason they treat us very well. We don't have to worry about any of those things. Everything, any permits that we need or anything like that, they all help us with. We have just been blessed as far as that goes.

Q: And how old is your brother?

A: Twenty-six.

Q: So you guys have been in business how long now?

A: We're going on now three years.

Q: So what do you think are the biggest mistakes that you have made thus far, the biggest lessons you've learned?

A: In some instances, getting in a little over our head, looking for...one of our mistakes has been like to order a lot of something to get a cheaper price and then realizing that you didn't really need that much anyway. But sometimes it comes back to save you at the end anyway, because maybe your cash flow is low one day and you can't make that order, but you have a whole bunch of it, so you don't need to make that order. So I guess it's pretty much our biggest mistake, ordering more than we need, even though it sometimes helps us.

Q: Any other major mistakes that you or your brother can pinpoint, even though you are young guys, some good lessons that you have learned thus far?

A: That's pretty much what it all comes down to. We've got vehicles right now. We have a delivery truck that we barely use, that we probably would have been better off using a logistical company, but we figured, hey, we'll get our own. Things like that. But at the same time they help you out, because you are independent, not depending on somebody else. Whenever we want, we can take our truck and use it for every purpose we need.

Q: Have you lost any significant money thus far?

A: I mean, like anybody, yeah. Investments into advertising and things like that. For example, with our previous company, we invested some money into advertising their product and we feel that that was a big loss, right there, because although we did make a little bit of money off that product, we would have made a whole lot more if we would have poured it into our own. So I guess you could say that is a big loss of money right there, in advertising.

Q: So did you feel like jumping off the Empire State Building?

A: I guess there are times that it can get that bad, but you can't really ever let it get that bad.

Q: What I'm really trying to pull out is the human dynamic—if you've made a mistake, how did you recover personally? Were you depressed? How did you get past that?

A: You just know that you have to do it. You have to. That's what it is. You can't quit. You have money owed. Bills are going to keep coming. You can't stop now. You have to just bounce back as soon as you can so that the loss doesn't become bigger.

Q: When we spoke on the phone, you said that you guys do things differently. What do you mean by differently?

A: I just think that there's a different mentality between people. It's what we were saying in the beginning when we were talking about it, and I see it within my own family, and with everybody that you deal with. When we first talk to someone and we say, "I'm about to do this" or "I'm about to do that," they are surprised. They go: "What? You're going to do what?" Sometimes they laugh. Sometimes they are just amazed at the fact: "Who? You? How is that possible?" They can't understand it—they're in that box. They just don't understand how you can be the one that provides the consumer. That's what this country is all about.

Ten percent of this country is rich beyond belief, and the other ninety, we're either doing horrible or just making it. And that's the way it is, so if you conform to that, you'll never get out of that ninety. You have to think differently. You have to get out of that. Believe that you can be in that ten percent. Why not? They're human. That's all it is.

Q: Are either one of you guys married?

A: No, not at all. We might as well be though, but no.

Q: When I started my own business, 25 years ago, the first thing I did, I lost my start-up capital. And when you suffer, you not only have economic consequences, but there are personal and social consequences, and as an entrepreneur, you have to go through all of that.

A: It's tough. You can take a lot of that home with you. And other people have to deal with it. But what are you going to do? This is the life we choose.

Q: You're 28 now. Where do you see yourself being at 48? What are your future plans and goals?

A: There's a lot of things that I want to do, but honestly at the end of it all, I just want to relax. That's all it comes down to: I don't want to have any worries.

Q: In business, are you trying to build a big distribution company? Are you trying to become the biggest distributor of this type of product? What are some of the things that are maybe just in the back of your mind?

A: In the back of my mind, the media. I would love to get involved with media somehow, just sell a product that costs nothing. That's what these media companies are involved in. But basically overall, I just want to be able to relax, have other people running what I have created. That's it.

Q: A lot of times people who start in one area end up in another area. For example, I think American Express started as a wire transfer service, now it's a big credit card service. Do you see any other possible scenarios where you could end up being the CEO of American Express or the CEO of this or that? I know this is all kind of futuristic.

A: Yeah, but you can never close the door on anything like that. If somebody else finds you valuable, and they are willing to give you what you want or envision, then maybe you can either partner with them or be involved with them in some way or somehow. I don't see why not.

Q: How do you see building generational wealth? You are like the second generation, right? How do you see building generational wealth for your kids or grandkids?

A: It's the only way for us to progress as minorities. If we don't start thinking that way, we're never going to get out of that rut. We have to think to pass it on, always pass it on.

As far as blacks and Hispanics and everything, Hispanics I guess are kind of the newest ones in here, but as far as African Americans as well, you can't really compare it to the Anglos in this country yet. We don't have as much time as they have in this country, but slavery was still, it's still part of this century, so we don't really have as much time like they do. We don't have that many generations.

I'm pretty sure you being African American, you may have somebody still alive in your family tree that was involved in slavery or something like that, and until we get far enough past that, we won't be able to reach the levels that they've reached off our sweat. The reason that a lot of the Anglos here are so wealthy is because of slavery and things that their grandparents and ancestors took advantage of, free labor, pretty much, and building empires off free labor. And now these institutions are already built. And they continue to run and generate profits. It doesn't matter that they have incurred costs now. They have created this wealth. But it's through generations. And we're still new here. The Anglos have ten generations, twelve generations here, and we don't have that. We're still on our second. So by the time we get to our fifth, sixth, we'll probably be further along than they were in their fifth or sixth, but it's still going to take about that long.

Q: I know when I was in business, I was competing against guys whose fathers started the business 60 years ago. So they had the expertise, they had the knowledge, and they had the money. I'm new. Nobody in my family has been in business before.

A: It's a major disadvantage that we are always going to have. Until we get a little further. Your kids may just slightly have to deal with it, and then your grandkids probably won't have to deal with it at all. These are problems that they won't understand.

Q: Then they get spoiled, right? So do you have any employees that work for you?

A: What we do is mostly we'll get employees as we need them. We don't have employees that we hire on a weekly basis, or on a daily basis or anything like that. Just as we need them, because we don't really run every day like that. We don't run that way. As far as our manufacturing side, we'll manufacture for a week out of the month.

Q: Where is your manufacturing facility?

A: We have it in another location right now.

Q: But it's in New York.

A: Yeah.

Q: So you have a warehouse facility and all that. Do you have a large inventory? If you are in 100 stores, how is your production set up to supply these various stores?

A: Basically what we do is we just make enough in that week of the manufacturing process to cover us for a good month or two months. Then we'll just do that every week until we don't have to run for a while because we're overstocked or whatever like that. We just make sure we have enough.

Q: So do you have to store a lot of inventory in your warehouse facility? The reason I ask is that a lot of people do what they call 'just-in-time delivery.' They have just enough. It goes straight to the customer so they don't have to warehouse it.

A: We'll warehouse some anyway, just in case we don't produce in time or whatever, we'll always have enough.

Q: Is that expensive?

A: Not really. It's usually a location you are going to have anyway, so you just stack it with the stuff and that's it. It's a one-time investment.

Q: Your business is regional right now; do you see expanding beyond that?

A: Of course, we want to go nationwide with it eventually.

Q: It's tricky to do that.

A: Oh yeah. There's a lot of things to it. It's what we're going to do.

Challenges As A Minority

Q: So do you think Hispanic businesspeople face more challenges than others? And if so, what kind of challenges?

A: I think that we're pretty much on the same field as the African Americans. We're all generalized the same. The other races all look at us the same way—we're all just minorities to them. So whatever obstacles there are for someone who is African American, it's pretty much the same obstacles that we have, except for the barrier of language in some aspects. But at the same time we are also more open to international business, whereas African Americans raised with English as their language, we usually have English and Spanish, which opens us to a whole other continent, and a lot of other places as well where Spanish is spoken, Europe, Spain is over there and it's all Spanish. We can communicate with them perfectly fine. All of South America practically. Even Brazil where they speak Brazilian, it's still similar to Spanish and we can communicate. So it helps us in some aspects, but in this country, it's pretty much the same.

Q: But do you find that when you try to go to these clients, these customers, does the fact that you're Hispanic…Do they now take you seriously or think you are—

A: Sometimes, yeah. Sometimes they feel there is somebody else behind you; that you are not capable of having done this all by yourself so there must be somebody else behind you, somebody Jewish or something, something different. Sometimes it's just in your best interest to let them believe that and just let it be, and sometimes you'll get representation from someone else that can actually get you the deal if you feel that it's going to inhibit you from accomplishing something. Get somebody involved. There are plenty of people who are willing to help you, for their own interest.

Q: What I found when I was trying to sell, even in government places, the buyers would often say, "Oh, I've been doing business with John Smith for 50 years." So even though you might have a product, you might have a good product, they won't even let you in the door because it's already been established.

A: It's tough. It is. But I've read that there are certain things where it works to help a bit. Like that railroad that they made over the Van Wyck—the Air Train—that it was a 300-million-dollar project and it was assigned to a certain contractor, but he had to give up a certain percent of that, I think it was like 20 percent of that, to minority-owned businesses and things like this. You don't get the whole pie, obviously, but you get to eat a little bit, and you get that 20 percent, maybe next time, you'll be in the running for that big contract.

Q: Most of those said they had to place a good faith effort for the 20 percent, meaning that they can say, if I can't find a qualified minority vendor, then I can take the whole 100 percent. There's where a lot of those things go down. I've seen it. Absolutely.

A: I don't doubt it that it would happen, but the thing is you can't be completely closed to it. There are opportunities. If you always think that there is going to be something to stop you, you are never going to do anything.

Q: The other side of that is that a lot of companies who want to do business with Hispanics and African Americans, they don't want to deal with like 10 or 15 Hispanic companies, or 10 or 15 African-American companies. They want some guy who is big enough to supply everything they need, so a bunch of little guys are trying to get a piece of that action, and it doesn't make sense from the buyer's standpoint, he wants one established company.

A: That's who we sell to. That little guy that sells to that other guy. That's what it is. You've got to take what you can. For whatever reason, your product breaks out of that mold, then they are forced to deal with you.

Q: So are you very active in business organizations or professional organizations?

A: Not really. We stick below the radar.

Q: You stay way below the radar. I interviewed another Hispanic guy and he is active in the Hispanic Chamber of Commerce, and it's good because it brings him business but I think you are in a whole other area, a whole different type of business.

A: Usually what we do is, as I said before, we'll deal with another guy or something like that. We're that guy behind the scenes. We work our things out.

Advice For New Entrepreneurs

Q: So as an old man of 28, going on 29, if you had a young person coming up behind you, what advice would you give them in terms of going into business?

A: First stop, go see Harry Wells. You've got to find the right people. You've got to find the right people to help you through things. We can easily get side-tracked and do things the wrong way. If you try to go on your own, you don't know as much about certain fields as somebody else that could help you out. Just be open to them. Look for help and be open to them.

Q: Anything else you would like to add that you think is important to say, because what I am trying to do, I'm trying to inspire people that are coming up after you, or after us, so anything else you might want to add that I didn't bring up?

A: Maybe if we had the interview a couple of years later, and I'm a little higher up the ladder, there will be a lot more to say. When I have encountered a little more adversity, more challenges, but up to now, I haven't really encountered that many problems. I've only been—this is my third year and I'm a young buck.

Q: Well, I wanted to interview somebody who is young to get their perspective too. In fact, I was thinking—I didn't know if your old business had tanked, gone bad on you and you were starting something new, so I was very interested in like, if you had these problems, what were the problems? All of this is a learning experience.

A: Yeah. We definitely learned a lot with what we did as far as the first product we got involved in. And we just took all that and now we're trying to get past all the mistakes that we made before, make sure we don't make it with our own product and so on and so forth. Now pretty much just working really for ourselves now.

Q: You say, mistakes you made with the other product. List the two or three major mistakes. I want to make sure I capture that.

A: One problem that we had was with smaller guys—really small guys—that were able to bring product from overseas in suitcases and things like that, small amounts. These are things that we didn't foresee. Somebody who operates out of their own car, and doesn't have any type of overhead or anything like that. Enough of them can give you some headaches. And it creates a big problem for someone who is involved in business and has overhead and all that. Someone who is just out there trying to make a quick dollar—it's fine for them because all they have to pay for is gas, but for us it was a big problem. So that's one of the mistakes that we made—we just overlooked that.

Q: What about manufacturers? Was your manufacturer any big problem? Were they reliable? Were they a pain in the butt?

A: Well, we found one manufacturer that we dealt with that was overcharging us so we ended up dealing with somebody else, but I guess that's just part of business—you just learn as you go. That's pretty much it—you just learn as you go.

SUMMARY

Juan Vargas and his brother, both of whom are still in their twenties, are truly remarkable entrepreneurs. They have been in their present business a scant three years, yet they have achieved a level of success that many others only dream about. Their success is directly attributable to their marketing skills and their ability to harness the necessary resources to serve as a manufacturer/distributor of a high-demand product.

By building their own brand identity and growing a network of smaller distributors, the Vargas brothers are working to expand their business beyond its current regional geographic to market their product nationally.

BLUEPRINT FOR GROWTH

The importance of small business to the United States' economy is indisputable. Small businesses allow entrepreneurs to seize opportunities for self-sufficiency that lead to meaningful, gratifying, empowered lives. The opportunity to grow is on the minds of many in this group. A great many entrepreneurs become restless after achieving some measure of stability; they become bored with the daily routine, and they need new challenges, new adventures.

Most of the companies interviewed here have roughly a three- to six-year track record and their mean revenue ranges from approximately 1–3 million dollars. On the average, they employ around twenty people. They are thus in a transitional stage, struggling to grow their businesses into more advanced, mid-size companies. In the words of one of the interviewees, her company had "hit a plateau" and she needs new opportunities.

The classic example of an entrepreneur seeking new challenges and growth is evidenced in the interview with Patrick Heaney. At the age of sixty, Patrick decided that the future of transportation was global trade. He therefore sold his very profitable trucking business and set his sights on China. After selecting a local partner, he opened an office there. In the past six years, they've established several very large accounts and plan to double their revenue in the next two years. Patrick states that if he was a little younger, he would move to China to take better advantage of this boom frontier.

Growth, however, will be problematic for many bootstrap entrepreneurs. Although it can be said that they have performed miracles—surviving when so many others fail—they must develop new skills and a different mindset. Their tenacity and ability to 'shake and bake' now become secondary attributes.

With insight gained through numerous conversations, workshops, and deep reflection about this transitional phase, I've developed a blueprint for growth to provide clarity and direction to help these entrepreneurs achieve their objectives and reach their full potential.

SEIZING NEW OPPORTUNITIES

Because so many of the new-generation entrepreneurs are minorities, potential opportunities abound in inner cities across the U.S. Many metropolitan areas have major development projects scheduled. In downtown Brooklyn, nearly 22 billion dollars are slated for development projects. In a recent meeting of black contractors in Chicago, the rebuilding of this old American city was called a black contractor's dream. One of the participants in that meeting recently told me that he is swamped with work and is also renovating and flipping buildings in targeted areas.

To seize this valuable opportunity for growth, developing a collective synergy and flexible thinking are essential. For example, for the upcoming NETS Stadium in Brooklyn, one study participant, a fast food franchise owner, is considering applying to become a vendor of hot dogs, beer, etc. In this proposed five-billion-dollar complex, fifteen percent of the new vendor opportunities are slated for minority businesses.

Another of the interviewed clients is in the process of securing a long-term lucrative contract from a large governmental agency for a project that supplements her core business. It will be a terrain that she has some familiarity with and has the experience to rapidly grasp the dynamics of the new marketplace. The potential exists for this new revenue stream to surpass present earnings.

MANAGED GROWTH

This drive to grow must be managed and focused. It should not be in a frenzy, where one becomes overextended and financially exposed. There are numerous cases of entrepreneurs jumping at so-called opportunities and enduring disastrous consequences. Several small business owners that I work with have rushed into purchasing real estate that they cannot afford to quickly renovate. After three years, one such project is still not off the ground, and the financial strain has led to credit and cash flow problems. In one extreme case, in what should have been one of the most recent minority business success stories in New York, the business had a tragic ending. This franchise owner was so busy speculating with real estate that he ignored the financing needs of his breadwinner. He was recently evicted from his premises.

SELF-EMPOWERMENT

During these interviews, most people pointed out that they have a good accountant to interpret and resolve critical financial issues. This is both good and troubling. It cannot be overstated that entrepreneurs must learn the language of business—to comprehend bottom line numbers. This is the first step toward emancipation. Since our interview, one participant's accountant abruptly resigned, leaving the client facing penalties with the Internal Revenue Service for non-filing and nonpayment of withholding taxes. It is another dire situation.

The entrepreneur's plea of ignorance is understandable but not sufficient. Although one might not understand all the concrete steps, it is imperative to have an overview, to be able to grasp the basic processes and principles. Continuous education to learn business basics is an absolute necessity.

A. G. Gaston, the high school dropout but premiere African-American businessman until the last quarter of the 20th century states, "I studied, read, listened attentively to the advice of auditors; I learned quickly to digest a profit and loss statement" (Jenkins and Hines 2004).

It is important to understand the numbers from not only a perceptional level, but also to move to a conceptual understanding of emerging trends and interconnections. This is an advantage that entrepreneurs from MBA programs with their sophisticated financial skills have over bootstrap builders. You'll note that only one client interviewed here is engaged in advanced study (MBA training). When asked why, her response was that she is attempting to understand how money works.

FIND PROFESSIONAL ASSISTANCE

Obtaining business growth necessitates that successful entrepreneurs seek out professionals and learn from them. In most mom-and-pop operations, there is an enormous reliance on a network of family and friends. In some respect this circle of close associates is very beneficial. For a cash-based business, one client documented that the daily revenue intake was much higher when a relative was behind the cash register.

For operational growth, more professional management is needed. It is tough convincing the small business owners that a professional manager would help alleviate setbacks, stress, and exhaustion. An exception to this stubbornness is Patrick Heaney. It is his strong conviction and practice that fast-track success depends on hiring good people and compensating them well. This has allowed him to concentrate on client development and lucrative accounts. His role is always selling and serving as the visionary catalyst for future growth.

If not able to hire professionals, entrepreneurs need to develop a relationship with consultants as an alternative, but many entrepreneurs turn a deaf ear to outside advice. They are headstrong, beating their chest and boasting that they brought the company to this point. In their view, many professionals are pencil pushers who have not 'been there, done that.' One specific example is a minority contractor that I'm familiar with who could drastically increase his revenue with better financial controls and internal administration. However, his very detailed rectification plan by a CPA was never implemented, nor seriously discussed.

Some entrepreneurs are also very cheap—penny wise and pound foolish. They have been spoiled by organizations like the Small Business Development Centers that provide free services.

In her dynamic book, *Diary of a Small Business Owner* (see Recommended Readings), Anita Brattina argues that developing an Advisory Board was paramount to her success. It took years of criticisms, nudging, and questioning by Board members before she understood and implemented their suggestions. Once she made a mental breakthrough, her business took a qualitative leap and became a 100-million-dollar annual operation. A comment made by Roy Sawyer in his interview was that a significant problem is that many business owners do not want to listen to others. He also stated that they must stop using any regular accountant and pay for the services of a CPA.

BIG FISH IN SMALL PONDS

In a recent television appearance by Bill Gates and Warren Buffet (the two richest people in the U.S.), both described how their initial partners contributed to their success story.

It is with great reservation that I raise the point that many entrepreneurs/small business owners should consider developing a relationship with a business partner for their future plans. This is complicated because many are adamantly opposed to this notion. After all, they built their company from scratch. One person I interviewed told me, quite forcefully, that this was out of the question.

Nevertheless, it is my belief that their ability to evolve into a larger entity will be enhanced by different skills, experiences, and viewpoints. It could be argued that one reason the U.S. business environment is so cutting edge and dynamic is because of the diversity in nationalities, opinions, and pragmatic suggestions for problem solving.

ECONOMY OF SCALE

The term 'economy of scale' is an important concept in economics. For our purpose, it will mean the pooling together of resources to increase productive capacity and make a breakthrough. Small contractors in particular will never win any significant contracts in major development projects as long as they remain small and financially impotent. In the retail arena, major retailers (i.e., Sears, JCPenney, etc.) are upfront about their desire to deal exclusively with minority suppliers of size and substance. It is not cost effective for them to deal with a network of scattered, small producers.

Technical service providers and small business organizations must encourage central planning initiatives and convince entrepreneurs: To build is strength in unity. Major projects must be tackled with a scaleable, fluid division of labor. Esley Porteous stated in his interview that his company could financially benefit from a relationship with minority civic and construction engineers. After our session, my subsequent conversation with a struggling minority engineering/contractor firm really piqued their interest in sprinkler projects as a possible strategic opportunity. Their combined experience, finances, collateral, and enhanced credit status will provide leverage to bid on upcoming sizable contracts.

Building the collective strength of minority contractors is no simple task. An outside technical/management agency must shepherd this process and become a driving, innovative force. It must play the leading role in developing a roadmap and building the membership of its congregation. Specialized training must be provided to subjects, ranging from business development to standards of job performance. There must also be guidance through the maze of applications, certification processes, and contractual conditions.

IN SUMMARY

Today's entrepreneurs—the new American pioneers—need to grow beyond their start-up capabilities and increase their capacity to produce in order to create a sustainable future for not only themselves and their families, but for their employees and employees' families as well. With a focused action plan in hand, it is possible for motivated entrepreneurs to continue blazing new trails for those coming up behind them. This will allow them, and their heirs, to take their rightful place among those currently enjoying the lifestyle known as the American Dream. This is, after all, the land of opportunity, and here, anything is possible.

RECOMMENDED READINGS

Bloomberg, Michael. *Bloomberg by Bloomberg*. New York: John Wiley & Sons, 1997.

Brattina, Anita F. *Diary of a Small Business Owner: A Personal Account of How I Built a Profitable Business*. New York: AMACOM, 1996.

Bygrave, William D. and Dan D'Heilly. *The Portable MBA in Entrepreneurship Case Studies*. New York: John Wiley & Sons, 1997.

Dell, Michael and Catherine Fredman. *Direct From Dell: Strategies that Revolutionized an Industry*. New York: HarperCollins, 1999.

Godin, Seth. *The Bootstrapper's Bible: How To Start and Build a Business With a Great Idea and (Almost) No Money*. Chicago: Dearborn, 1998.

Hess, Kenneth L. *Bootstrap: Lessons Learned Building a Successful Company from Scratch*. Carmel (CA): S-Curve Press, 2001.

Jenkins, Carol and Elizabeth Gardner Hines. *Black Titan: A.G. Gaston and the Making of a Black American Millionaire*. New York: One World, 2004.

Kawasaki, Guy. *The Art of the Start: The Time-Tested, Battle-Hardened Guide for Anyone Starting Anything*. New York: Penguin, 2004.

Krass, Peter. *The Book of Entrepreneurs' Wisdom: Classic Writings by Legendary Entrepreneurs*. New York: John Wiley & Sons, 1999.

Orfalea, Paul and Ann Marsh. *Copy This!: Lessons from a Hyperactive Dyslexic who Turned a Bright Idea Into One of America's Best Companies*. New York: Workman Publishing, 2005.

Steinfeld, Jake. *I've Seen a Lot of Famous People Naked, and They've Got Nothing on You! Business Secrets from the Ultimate Street-Smart Entrepreneur*. New York: AMACOM, 2006.

If you have enjoyed this book and would like more information, please visit the following website:

HarryLWells.com
Or check out my Blog at
www.wellspokenentrepreneur.blogspot.com

978-0-595-41430-7
0-595-41430-3

www.ingramcontent.com/pod-product-compliance
Lightning Source LLC
Chambersburg PA
CBHW031050180526
45163CB00002BA/762